Sharable Parables

by

Steven James

Standard
PUBLISHING
Bringing The Word to Life™

Cincinnati, Ohio

DEDICATION
To the pastor in Illinois who showed me The Way

THANKS & ACKNOWLEDGMENTS

In the late 1990s I was speaking at a camp in Minnesota, and one of the staff members, a college student, told me about having kids act out one of Jesus' stories. She called it a "Sharable Parable." I can't remember if we actually acted out a story or not that day, but the phrase stuck in my mind. The title for this book came from that conversation. So to that young lady, whoever she is, my thanks go out to you!

I'd also like to thank my daughters for being such willing guinea pigs for my ideas; Liesl Huhn, Dana Standridge, Christina Wallace, and Quinne Bryant for their incredibly helpful suggestions; Mark Collins for his theological insights and research; Ruth Frederick, Paul Learned, and Bruce Stoker for believing in this project; Pamela Harty, for encouraging me every step of the way; Doe River Gorge for giving me a quiet place to write when I needed it most; Mrs. Poe's and Mrs. Chambers's classes of 2004 at Providence Academy, for helping me test-drive these stories; and finally, to the folks who have attended my storytelling seminars, workshops, and conferences over the years. Your ideas, creativity, and energy were inspiring. I couldn't have written this book without you.

Standard Publishing, Cincinnati, Ohio.
A division of Standex International Corporation.

Edited by Christina Wallace
Cover design by Joel Armstrong
Cover illustrations by Paula Becker
Interior design by Ed Koehler

12 11 10 09 08 07 06 05   5 4 3 2 1

ISBN 0-7847-1632-3

Earlier versions of brief sections of this book first appeared in *The Creative Storytelling Guide* (Standard Publishing, 2002). The material has been adapted, expanded, and reworked for inclusion in this book. Used by permission.

TABLE OF CONTENTS

Introduction

Long ago, Truth and Parable were talking.

"I just don't get it," complained Truth. "Nobody listens to me. Everywhere I go, people avoid me, turn their backs on me, or laugh at me! I can't get my message across if people won't hear me out!"

"Well," said Parable, "I hate to be the one to point this out to you, but . . . um . . . well, you don't have any clothes on, Truth! You're the Naked Truth. . . . It turns people off! Dress yourself up a little bit. I mean, look at me. People are always complimenting me on how sharp I look!"

Sure enough, Parable did have a pretty cool outfit on.

And so, Truth went to the store. He didn't know exactly what kind of clothes to get (since he'd never worn them before), so he decided to buy the same kind of clothes as Parable.

The next day as he was walking down the street, someone said, "Hey, Parab—oh, it's you, Truth. Well, nice outfit . . ."

And for the first time, someone actually listened to what Truth had to say. People didn't turn away and laugh. And they weren't so offended by Truth anymore.

And ever since then, Truth and Parable have been good friends. In fact, some people say that even to this very day, wherever you find Parable, you'll find Truth standing right there by his side. *

Jesus knew that people learn best through stories. That's why, when he spoke to the crowds, *"he did not say anything to them without using a parable" (Mark 4:34)*. Jesus was a storyteller.

And he has chosen us—you and me—to pass his story on to the next generation.

Just as Jesus spoke in parables, so we continue to speak in parables to share his stories of faith so that . . .

. . . the next generation might know them—even the children not yet born—that they in turn might teach their children. So each generation can set its hope anew on God, remembering his glorious miracles and obeying his commands.
                                                                              (Psalm 78:6, 7 NLT)

But how do we do it? How do we take Jesus' timeless and life-transforming tales and retell them so that they connect with the hearts and minds of twenty-first century children?

That's what this book is all about.

The ideas in these pages will equip you to tell the stories of Jesus creatively and effectively. You'll be able to better understand his parables, retell them in engaging ways, and help your students apply them to their lives. You'll discover:

1. Background information that'll help your listeners picture the stories as you tell them.
2. Interactive activities that'll help engage your students while you speak.
3. Creative ways of retelling the parables so that those who have heard them before can see the stories in a new light.
4. Other stories that reinforce the main point of the parables.
5. Application ideas that'll help the students put the truths of the stories into practice.

What do I need to know to get started?

When telling Bible stories, it's important to rely on the power and presence of the Holy Spirit rather than upon your own cleverness or eloquence (see 1 Corinthians 2:1-5). We want to grow fruit that will last for an eternity, not just make an impression that will last until the next show starts on TV.

Also, pray for your ability to reach your listeners. Never underestimate the power of prayer to move God and the power of God to change lives. Our goal is simply to speak the truth in a way that moves people to the place where they can encounter God.

While you're welcome to read this book all the way through, cover to cover, you might find it more helpful to glance through the book to familiarize yourself with the content and layout, and then flip to the story you're preparing to tell. Start there and see where it leads you. Each chapter is designed to stand alone. However, it will be helpful for you to read all the chapters at some point,

*Based on an eighteenth-century Jewish folktale.

since each one includes unique ideas that you can adapt to nearly any parable.

Each story has its own challenges. There isn't one right way to approach every story. For that reason, I've tried to shape each chapter around the specific nature of each unique story, while still including certain information in each chapter for consistency.

You may also find it helpful to glance through the Scripture Verse Index, the Topical Index, or the Storytelling Technique Index found in the back of the book. These appendices will help you find just the right story for your lesson or event.

Special Features

I wanted to create a book that would be easy to use, informative, and practical. So in each chapter I've included:

1. **Gospel Connection** - Sometimes it's easy to forget to emphasize God's grace and just tell stories that teach moral lessons. These reminders draw attention back to the heart of the gospel to help you keep the main thing the main thing.

2. **Memory Sparks** - These memory sparks will help you think of stories from your own life that relate to the story you're planning to tell. Connecting on a personal level with the stories you tell is essential to retelling them with passion, sincerity, and authenticity.

3. **QuickTips** - These brief storytelling tips will help you improve your rapport with the audience and increase your expertise at learning and sharing stories.

4. **W.E.G.I.** (Weird & Extremely Goofy Ideas) - These optional ideas will help educators who have a childlike heart playfully engage their students in ways that sometimes get wet, wild, and weird! These ideas will be especially popular with those hard-to-reach preteens!

5. **Creative Connection Section** - Sometimes all you need is a nudge in the right direction. The interactive ideas in this section will help spark your creative juices and help you teach and tell your story in a more active and engaging way.

There are lots of scripts and skits in this book. With the purchase of this book, you receive photocopy permission to make enough copies of them for your students to use in your classroom.

Nearly all of the ideas in this book can be adapted to meet the learning needs of children at different ages or places on the developmental continuum. However, each chapter includes specific ideas for retelling stories to younger children (ages 3–7) and to older ones (ages 8–12) to help you more easily reach your students.

> ### QuickTip #1 - Stay on Track.
> When you tell a story, tell the story! Don't let it morph into a history lesson, a morality lecture, or a series of mini-sermons. Some people spend more time explaining what a story is going to be about (or what the story was about) than they do telling the story!
>
> So if your introduction to a story is longer than the story, you've probably got a few changes to make!

HOW CAN I BETTER UNDERSTAND THESE PARABLES?

When the disciples asked Jesus why he spoke in parables, he answered in a riddle:

Though seeing, they do not see; though hearing, they do not hear or understand.
(Matthew 13:13)

Jesus told parables to reveal truth to those seriously seeking it and to conceal truth from those who were not.

How can parables do that? Well, the word *parable* comes from a Greek word that means "to throw or place together." A parable is a way of placing one story next to another so that spiritual or moral truth can be taught.

Stories are incredibly powerful tools for teaching. As Robert Atkinson wrote in his book *The Gift of Stories*, "Stories—those that have been told across the generations, as well as our own—inform, inspire, teach, maintain moral codes, record events that become history, establish family lines and genealogy, preserve customs, guide us, show us possibilities, open our hearts, make us laugh, and clarify all aspects of life while healing and transforming."[1]

> ### QuickTip #2 - One-Point Sermons?
> Don't try to preach three-point sermons to kids. Instead, take a cue from Jesus. As far as I can tell, Jesus never once taught a three-point sermon. Instead, he shared one-point sermons. And most of the time, he didn't even tell people what the point was! Just tell a series of stories that all relate to a central theme, and then, if necessary, show people the thread of meaning that weaves its way through them all.
> When presenting a story program for children, tell a story, preach for a minute. Tell a story, preach for a minute—not the other way around!

To understand a parable, remember to look at it in context. Look at the verses following and preceding the parable to understand who the audience was and what led up to the telling of the story.

For example, Luke 18:1 says, *"Then Jesus told his disciples a parable to show them that they should always pray and not give up."* This verse tells us who Jesus told the story to and precisely why it was told! If you were to teach this story without reading this verse, you could easily misunderstand the entire point of the parable of "The Persistent Widow"!

Be sure to take the time to really study each story carefully before telling it. You might be surprised by what you find!

Most of Jesus' stories teach more than one single, specific point. Maybe that's why he didn't like explaining them to his listeners. He wanted people to engage with the story where they were. And sometimes people who were at different places in their journeys of faith got different things out of his stories.

> ### QuickTip #3 - The Icing on the Liver?
> When you tell a joke or a story, make sure the whole tale is engaging and that people don't have to put up with a dull story just to get to a satisfying ending. The punch line should be the icing on the cake, not the icing on the liver!

The point is, take the time to study the story carefully yourself so that you can make sure you're being faithful when you retell it. When we stand before God one day, he isn't going to ask us if we've been faithful in teaching a certain curriculum or lesson plan, but he will ask us if we've been faithful in teaching his Word.

Do I have to memorize these stories?

In a word, no. The goal of storytelling is not to recite a script accurately; it's to tell a story effectively. So, rather than concentrate on getting the words right, concentrate on helping your listeners connect with the story.

The ideas in this book are simply suggestions. Yes, they might work exactly as they appear, but many factors affect how a story should be told: the age of your listeners . . . their maturity . . . their ability to pay attention . . . the number of children in the room . . . the size of the room . . . the seating arrangement . . . the lighting and sound of the room . . . the number of distractions and other things going on . . . the flow of the lesson . . . the energy level of your listeners . . . their prior positive or negative experiences listening to stories . . . whether or not the kids have had breakfast . . . or even when the last rest room break occurred!

As you can see, the social setting in which storytelling takes place has much to do with the ability of your listeners to pay attention. When you tell a story, you need to take those factors into account. Do your best to remove distractions and provide an environment that's conducive to listening to stories. Then, be ready to adapt your story so you really connect with your listeners.

Spend enough time preparing your story so that it flows naturally, but don't practice a story so much that is ends up sounding canned or packaged.

---

[1] *The Gift of Stories* by Robert Atkinson. Bergin & Garvey, Westport, Connecticut. 1995 page 3.

Actually, there's no single right way to tell any story! Matthew, Mark, Luke, and John all tell the story of Jesus' life, yet they all tell it differently and from different perspectives. So . . . which one of them is right?

Well, they're all right! Yet they are each *unique*. As different people telling the story to different audiences, they naturally tell the story differently. They emphasize different things and take great care to use the language and narrative structure that will best impact their specific group of listeners.

When you set out to tell the stories of Jesus, try to do the same. Strive to be faithful to use your own unique personality and giftedness to tell his story in your own uniquely personal way, just like the Gospel writers did.

HOW MUCH SHOULD I CHANGE JESUS' STORIES WHEN I RETELL THEM?

There are certainly times and places for memorizing Bible stories; indeed, God told his people to think about his words night and day, at home and away (Deuteronomy 6:6-9)! His Word should be in our heads, on our hearts, and on our lips. Memorizing and then reciting Bible stories can be very effective. But it shouldn't be the only teaching technique you use.

When you retell the parables of Jesus, it's your job to translate them into the language of today so that the stories of Jesus can reach the hearts, minds, and imaginations of your listeners. Most kids today don't know what a denarius is, or what a mustard seed looks like, or how much a talent is worth. Jesus used familiar references and images in his stories. He told stories about farmers and fishermen . . . seeds and sheep . . . vineyards and pigs . . . and fishing nets and pearl merchants. People in his day were familiar with all of those things, but many of us today are not.

Sometimes you have to rephrase Jesus' stories just so kids can understand them!

In addition, most of Jesus' stories are very brief. Actually, they're more like plot summaries than fleshed-out stories. For example, while telling a series of short stories about the kingdom of Heaven, Jesus said:

> *The kingdom of heaven is like treasure hidden in a field. When a man found it, he hid it again, and then in his joy went and sold all he had and bought that field. Again, the kingdom of heaven is like a merchant looking for fine pearls. When he found one of great value, he went away and sold everything he had and bought it.*
>
> *(Matthew 13:44-46)*

Here, in less than 70 words, Jesus told two stories. It would take you less than a minute to retell them both. So what are we to do? Simply tell the story word for word and then move on? Well, you could, but that would be an awfully short lesson!

We certainly need to be faithful in retelling God's story. We don't change it around just to include the stuff we're comfortable with, to leave out the things we don't like, or to make it mean something other than what Jesus intended. No way! That's the *opposite* of what we want to do!

Instead, we want to be faithful in telling the stories so that our listeners can understand them, picture them, and be impacted by them.

Help students understand Jesus' stories

If it's our goal to share God's story with twenty-first-century children, then we need to use the language they understand. That's what Jesus did with his listeners. He spoke in the words they knew and used examples and stories they understood. When we attempt to teach his stories to children of today, we can follow the example of Jesus.

Use kid-friendly language when telling your story, and rephrase the stories when necessary to make them more approachable and understandable.

Help students picture Jesus' stories

Many parables are very brief, taking less than a minute to retell. When you tell them you'll need to add details so your students can picture them in their minds.

Other stories go on for many chapters, or even books, of the Bible. You'll need to condense those stories so children can follow and understand them.

Strive to be faithful as you adapt the story, but don't worry about memorizing the exact words.

Help students be impacted by Jesus' stories

Many Bible stories include cultural events and contextual ideas that people in the twenty-first-century don't understand. Unfortunately, too often when Bible teachers explain the relevance of the events, the story turns into a history lesson. By weaving explanations into the story itself, we can engage *as well as* inform our listeners as the story is told.

> **QuickTip #6 - Questions, Questions, and More Questions!**
> Rather than ask review questions that simply restate the obvious, ask questions that challenge your students to look for ways to relate the story to their lives. Jesus often did this when he told stories. He asked thought-provoking questions that helped his listeners discover the point of the story for themselves.
>
> Avoid asking questions that everyone already knows the answer to. Instead, strive to ask questions that will challenge both you and your students to think about the theme of the story in a new light!

So, it's OK to look for ways to translate Jesus' stories into words and images that children of today can identify with and easily apply to their lives.

Strive to be faithful in discerning and conveying the heart of the story, but don't get tangled up trying to do everything word for word!

If you teach the same group of students each week, it's easy to forget which stories, illustrations and ideas you've used. Photocopy and use the following chart to keep track of what story you told, what ideas you used, and suggestions for future programs.

Chapter/Story:
Ideas used:
Date performed:
Description of my listeners:
Here's what I'd change . . .
Here are some new ideas I'd like to try . . .

The Wise and Foolish Builders 1

BASED ON: Matthew 7:21-29 and Luke 6:46-49

BIG IDEA: Those who don't put God's Word into practice won't be able to weather the storms of life.

GOSPEL CONNECTION: Rather than building our lives on our own opinions and principles, we need to build our lives on the precious Word of God. Submitting to Christ is the only pathway to true freedom:

> *See to it that no one takes you captive through hollow and deceptive philosophy, which depends on human tradition and the basic principles of this world rather than on Christ.* (Colossians 2:8)

> *The mind of sinful man is death, but the mind controlled by the Spirit is life and peace.* (Romans 8:6)

TOPICS: Following God, God's Word, hypocrisy, obedience, persecution, perseverance, wisdom

MEMORY SPARKS: To find yourself in this story, think of a time when . . .
1. You didn't follow the instructions and something terrible happened . . .
2. You saw how someone who'd obeyed Jesus for a long time was able to weather one of life's storms . . .
3. In the aftermath of a bad decision, you realized that God's rules are there to protect and provide for us, not to punish or limit us . . .

To help your students connect with this story, say, "Think of a time when . . ."
1. You broke a rule and got into trouble . . .
2. You didn't listen to your parents and ended up getting hurt . . .
3. You knew what you were supposed to do, but you did the opposite instead . . .

HERE'S WHAT'S GOING ON:

This story happens at the beginning of Jesus' ministry (right after he chose the 12 disciples) and at the end of Jesus' most famous sermon—the Sermon on the Mount.

To find out who Jesus is speaking to, you need to go back to Matthew 5:1, 2. Jesus has been followed by a large crowd, then his disciples arrive, and he begins to teach them. It's difficult to say whether Jesus' words were addressed just to his followers or more generally to the crowds of people. However, it is clear from the content of the Sermon on the Mount that his words are *at least* meant to apply to the lives of his followers. Either way, this story is aimed at those who hear God's Word and don't do it:

> *Not everyone who says to me, "Lord, Lord," will enter the kingdom of heaven, but only he who does the will of my Father who is in heaven.* (Matthew 7:21)

> *Why do you call me, "Lord, Lord," and do not do what I say? I will show you what he is like who comes to me and hears my words and puts them into practice.* (Luke 6:46, 47)

Hypocrites are those who say they love Jesus, and talk to God as if they are his children, and yet refuse to do what he says. Certainly we all fail. We're all human. But hypocrisy isn't the same as inconsistency. Hypocrites say one thing *with no intention of carrying it out.*

HERE'S WHAT THE STORY'S ABOUT:

Contrary to popular opinion, this story isn't about Jesus being the rock of our salvation. Nor is it about how to get to Heaven by trusting in Christ.

A careful reading of the story reveals that there's only one difference between the wise man (who built on the rock) and the foolish man (who built on the sand)—*the foolish man* didn't *put Jesus' words into practice, and the wise man* did. That's the only difference. They both heard the words. They both understood the words. Apparently, they both believed the words. But only one man put them into practice.

The key isn't just to know God's Word, or simply to understand God's Word, or even just to believe in God. As James points out, even the demons believe that! (See James 2:19.) The key to avoiding disaster is putting Jesus' words into practice.

Remember, these are Jesus' closing thoughts at the Sermon on the Mount. He's been teaching the people this whole new way of living, and now he says, "If you don't put this stuff into practice, you'll regret it." It makes total sense!

We can avoid lots of hardships and disasters if we live according to the teachings of Jesus. Obedience doesn't save us (God's grace alone does that), but obedience does help us avoid a disastrous life brought about by the consequences of sin.

You've seen it happen, haven't you? Someone knows all about right and wrong; but he doesn't put Christ's teachings into practice, and his choices come back to haunt him . . . he becomes addicted to alcohol or another drug . . . he gets entangled in an affair . . . he doesn't respect authority and ends up with a speeding ticket.

James, the brother of Jesus, emphasized the same point:

> *Therefore, get rid of all moral filth and the evil that is so prevalent and humbly accept the word planted in you, which can save you. Do not merely listen to the word, and so deceive yourselves. Do what it says.* (James 1:21, 22)

If we don't put Jesus' words into practice and live out our faith, there will be negative consequences in our lives. That's what this story is all about.

We have no right to call Jesus our Lord if we're not willing to put his teachings into practice.

QuickTip #7 - Remove Distractions!

It's true that young children are easily distracted, but don't underestimate the attention span of your students. Often we assume that they have a "short attention span" when the problem is usually that they have a "large *distraction* span!"

So be sure to remove distracting sights, sounds, smells, and activities before you begin your story. Make sure children can easily see and hear you as you tell your story. It'll help them pay attention and remember the lesson.

TELLING THIS STORY TO STUDENTS AGES 3-7

This story is a warning that if we believe in Jesus and don't obey what he says, bad things will happen. Help your students understand that in this story, "building on the rock" means "obeying God's Word." In essence, we need to live out our faith.

Preschool students want to have fun, be active, and won't understand elaborate analogies and metaphors about what rocks and storms and houses represent. So take the time to make the connection for them: **"If you do what God says, you'll be ready when hard times come!"** [1]

Younger students will also enjoy any ways you can come up with for engaging their squirmy little bodies into the message. For example, as you prepare to tell the story, invite the students on an **imaginary journey** to pretend they're getting ready for the storm. (You may wish to have a spray bottle of water, a fan, and a helper available before beginning this story!) For example . . .

> **Today's story will be lots of fun. Let's get ready to hear it . . .**
> **Oh, no! It looks like it's gonna rain outside! Quick everyone, shut the door!**
> *(as you go through these activities, act them out)* . . . **Close the windows . . . Grab a warm blanket and wrap yourself up in it . . . Can you feel the wind blow?** *(if desired, have a helper turn on a fan and aim it at the students)* . . . **Make the sound of a mighty wind! . . . Oh, no! Here comes the lightning!** . . . *(have a helper flicker the lights in your room)* . . .
> **And the thunder!** . . . *(have your helper make loud, scary sounds)* . . . **Is everyone safe from the storm? Good! . . . Here comes the water! Catch some raindrops on your tongues** . . . *(if desired, have your helper spray water at the children)* . . . **OK! Now, let's find out what's going on in Jesus' story . . . Let's see if our house can stand up to this storm!** . . .

After this activity, have someone read or tell the story of "The Wise and Foolish Builders." On the following page is a suggested way to retell this parable using a **storymime**. You could lead this by yourself, saying and doing all of the parts, or have a partner lead the students in performing the actions while you read or tell the story!

You may wish to think of other creative ways of having the students help you recreate the storm, the wind, and the waves. Consider handing them colored crepe paper to wave above their heads, fans to flutter in the air, or blue blankets to ripple as the waters rise . . .

For a good follow-up activity, let the children use fingerpaints and draw pictures of the two houses—one on sand, and the other on a great big rock. Or draw with frosting and pudding (either on wax paper or graham crackers) and sprinkle the drawings with candy. Then lick your home when the storm arrives!

> ## QuickTip #8 - Simon Says, "Put It into Practice!"
> Since this story is really about following directions, any game in which you have to listen carefully to directions and then put them into practice would help apply this story. For example, playing "Simon Says!" would show your students the importance of not just knowing what to do, but actually doing it!

[1] An earlier version of some of the material in this chapter first appeared in the 2001 Children's Ministry Seminar, "Fill 'Em Up" published by the International Network of Children's Ministry. Copyright 2001. All rights reserved. Used by permission.

The House on the Rock

(a storymime of "The Wise and Foolish Builders")

What to say:	What to do:
Today's story is about two builders.	Pretend to hammer a wall.
The first one is smart.	Tap your head and say, "Hm . . ."
The other one is a bit of a fool!	Look stupid and say, "Duh."
One day, the wise man went out to build his house . . .	Walk in place.
(Now, he's like those who hear God's Word . . .	Pull your ear.
. . . and DO what it says.)	Two thumbs up.
The wise man dug down deep.	Dig.
Until he found solid stone.	Knock on the floor and say, "Cool!"
He carried his boards . . .	Pick up some heavy boards.
He sawed the planks . . .	Saw the planks . . .
He hammered the walls . . .	Hammer 'em.
And he finished forming his house!	Draw a house in the air with your fingers.
Soon, a storm came! The rains fell . . .	Make your fingers into raindrops.
The rivers rose . . .	Pretend to swim.
The winds blew . . .	Say, "Whoosh!" and wave your arms around.
But the house on the rock stood firm.	Put your hands on your hips and stand like Superman.
Then, the man who wasn't so smart . . .	Look stupid and say, "Duh."
(Now, he's like people who hear God's Word,	Pull your ear.
. . . but don't put it into practice!)	Two thumbs down.
. . . went out to build his house . . .	Walk in place.
He didn't dig down deep to find a good base for his house.	Wave your hands back and forth and shake your head no!
He just started building right there on the beach by all the sunbathers.	Put on some suntan lotion and relax in the sun.
He carried his boards . . .	Pick up some heavy boards.
He sawed the planks . . .	Saw the planks . . .
He hammered the walls . . .	Hammer 'em.
And finished forming his house!	Draw a house in the air with your fingers.
Soon, a storm came! The rains fell . . .	Make your fingers into raindrops.
The rivers rose . . .	Pretend to swim.
The winds blew . . .	Say, "Whoosh!" and wave your arms around.
And the moment they did, his house fell with a great crash!	Fall over.
And when the people heard Jesus tell that story, they were amazed!	Stand up and be amazed.
For the digging is the doing,	Dig.
The foundation is the WORD.	Put your hands on your hips and stand like Superman.
'Cause the key to building wisely	Tap your head and nod.
Is to practice what you HEARD.	Cup your hand behind your ear.
If you claim to be a friend of Christ	Lift your hands toward Heaven.
But don't do what he SAID,	Shake your finger like a scolding teacher.
Your life won't stand forever	Hands on hips, shake your head no.
But will crumble down INSTEAD.	Fall over.
The end.	Take a bow.

Creative Connection Section		
Field Trip Ideas	It seems from Matthew 5:1 and Luke 6:17 that Jesus was on a level area of a mountainside when he told this story. So consider telling this story on a hillside or a mountain. Also, the story itself occurs on a beach, so telling it on a beachfront or seaside would be appropriate.	
Mood and Atmosphere	Setting for the storyteller	A cool, breezy mountainside.
	Setting for the story	A windy, rainy beach.
Sensory Connections	Sight	Place hammers, nails, boards, tools, and other construction items in the classroom to add to the construction site atmosphere. Wear a tool belt and pull your props out of a toolbox!
	Touch	Hand out building blocks and let the students build towers on different surfaces.
	Hearing	Use an umbrella to cue the audience. Have them make sound effects whenever you open it and be quiet to listen whenever you close it!
	Taste	Waves rushing against a house could be salty or fresh. Consider putting salt water and fresh water in spritz bottles and spraying the kids. Have them guess by the taste if the water is from the sea or the sky!
	Smell	Rain and storms often bring fresh, clean, moist smells. Buy different air fresheners and spray them in the room as you tell the story. (Use one for the <u>storm</u>, another for the <u>winds</u>, a third for the <u>stream</u>.) Use a fan to clear the air between each spritz!
Costume Ideas	You could dress up like a carpenter or construction worker to tell this story. Or wear a raincoat and pretend you're a TV news announcer sent to interview the two builders!	
Other Ideas	Make up a skit about a couple of people who go camping. They both know that it might rain up in the mountains, but only one of them decides to put up his tent. Bring a real camping tent and have one of the actors put it up. The other guy just drapes a net (or something else that won't give him any protection) over himself. Then, after they're both asleep, have someone sneak onstage with three buckets—two of them filled with water and one filled with confetti. Throw one bucket of water on the unprotected guy and one on the tent (make sure it's a waterproof tent!). Then take the bucket of confetti and toss it on the audience. At first, the kids will think that bucket is filled with water too!	

TELLING THIS STORY TO STUDENTS AGES 8-12

Elementary-age students will enjoy being actively involved in the story. They love surprises and having fun, so make the story interesting and exciting!

Invite them to make **sound effects** for the storm with their hands as you retell the story. By having the children tap their fingers, clap their hands, or pat their legs, you can produce the sound of thunder and rain. Get louder and softer as the storm comes closer or goes farther away. Or involve them in the storytelling with the following **reader's theatre** folktale that relates to Jesus' story.

The Three Little Oinkers
(a reader's theatre folktale for use with "The Wise and Foolish Builders")

Notes for the storytellers: Be sure to let PIG #3 look over his part before starting. He has some really big words to pronounce, and he needs to say those lines quickly! You'll need 6 children for this skit: NARRATOR (girl or boy), PIG #1 (girl or boy), PIG #2 (girl or boy), PIG #3 (preferably a boy), MAMA PIG (girl), BIG BAD WOLF (boy).

Consider having the children wear silly costumes, signs telling who they are, or plastic pig noses! Position the NARRATOR and MAMA PIG on the left side of the stage; PIG #1, PIG #2, and PIG #3 in the center; and the BIG BAD WOLF on the right side of the stage.

After photocopying and handing out the scripts, have each reader circle or highlight all of his speaking lines. This will help everyone know when to say their parts.

Give MAMA PIG a nice big wig! You'll also need one clothespin for each of the pigs. Bring up the stage lights, and then begin when the listeners are quiet.

TEACHER:	**Lights! . . . Camera! . . . Action!**
NARRATOR:	**Once upon a time, there were three little oinkers.**
PIG #1:	*(shyly)* **I'm oinker number one . . .**
PIG #2:	*(stuck-up)* **I'm piglet number two. Don't call me an oinker!**
PIG #3:	*(like a tough guy)* **Yo. I'm oinker number three. You got a problem wi' dat?! Huh?!**
NARRATOR:	**One day, their mother—**
MAMA PIG:	**—That's me!—**
NARRATOR:	**—gave them instructions on how to build their houses.**
MAMA PIG:	**I'm an architect—**
NARRATOR:	**—So that they'd be safe from the Big Bad Wolf.**
WOLF:	**That's me. I'm a carnivore.**
MAMA PIG:	**Now, piggies—**
ALL PIGS:	*(together)* **Yeah, Ma?**
MAMA PIG:	**When you build your house, use the best and strongest materials.**
ALL PIGS:	*(together)* **But why, Ma?**
MAMA PIG:	**So the Big Bad Wolf can't get you.**
WOLF:	**I'll get 'em anyway.**
NARRATOR:	**And so, off they went—**
ALL PIGS:	*(together)* **Bye, Ma! . . .** *(singing)* **We're off to see the Wizard! The wonderful Wizard of Oz—**
NARRATOR:	**Um, that's not what they were singing.**

PIG #2:	Oh . . .
ALL PIGS:	*(together, singing)* **Hi-ho! Hi-ho! It's off to build we go . . .**
NARRATOR:	**Um . . . no.**
PIG #3:	**Oh . . .** *(rapping, with rhythm)* **Yo! . . . I'm a tough, tough piggy don't mess with ME! I'm gonna build a house and you will SEE! It'll keep me safe when I close the DOOR! So the Big Bad Wolf won't come no MORE!**
ALL PIGS:	*(together)* **So the Big Bad Wolf won't come no MORE!**
NARRATOR:	**Well, close enough . . . So, the first little oinker went to build his house.**
PIG #1:	*(timidly)* **Hm . . . I know my Mama said to use the best building materials, but they cost too much. I don't wanna pay that much. I think I'll use straw instead.**
MAMA PIG:	**You're gonna regret it!**
NARRATOR:	**So he built his house out of straw. And soon, the Big Bad Wolf came.**
WOLF:	**I'm Big!**—
NARRATOR:	**—That's right.**
WOLF:	**I'm Bad!**—
NARRATOR:	**—Uh-huh.**
WOLF:	**I'm Mr. Wonderful!**—
NARRATOR:	**Oh, brother.**
WOLF:	**Little oinker! Little oinker! Let me in!**
PIG #1:	*(shyly)* **Not by the hair on my chinny, chin, chin!**

WOLF:	**Then I'll huff and I'll puff and I'll bring you DEATH, 'Cause I got the world's worst morning BREATH!**
NARRATOR:	**So he huffed and puffed.**
WOLF:	*(blow in PIG #1's face . . .)*
PIG #1:	**Whew! . . . You weren't kidding!**
NARRATOR:	**And he knocked down the house.**
WOLF:	**Cool.**
PIG #1:	**Uh-oh.**
NARRATOR:	**And that first little oinker went to his brother's house.**
PIG #2:	**That's me.**
NARRATOR:	**He had built his house out of—**
PIG #2:	**Licorice.**
NARRATOR:	**What? No. He built his house out of sticks.**
PIG #2:	**Yes, licorice sticks.**
NARRATOR:	**Oh, brother.**
PIG #2:	**Licorice is cheaper and easier to use. And besides, it's yummy!**
NARRATOR:	**And up came the Big Bad Wolf.**
WOLF:	**I'm Big!**—
NARRATOR:	**—Oh, no.**
WOLF:	**I'm Bad!**—
NARRATOR:	**—Not this again.**
WOLF:	**I'm Mr. Marvelous!**
NARRATOR:	**Oh, give me a break.**

WOLF:	Little oinkers! Little oinkers! Let me in!
PIGS #1 & #2:	Not by the hair on our chinny, chin, chins!
WOLF:	Then I'll huff and I'll puff and I'll bring you DEATH, 'Cause I got the world's worst morning BREATH!
NARRATOR:	So he huffed and puffed. And he knocked down the house.
WOLF:	*(blow in PIG #2's face . . .)*
PIG #2:	Whew! And the pigs too.
PIG #1:	That was some kind of bad breath . . .
WOLF:	Cool.
NARRATOR:	And both of those pigs went to their older brother's house.
PIG #3:	Yo, that's me. I'm oinker number three.
NARRATOR:	He had built his house out of—
PIG #3:	*(quickly)* —Superior grade, high alloy, drop-forged, non-oriented, silicon, fully processed steel with reinforced, rebar support beams and a high-level, load-bearing-capacity concrete base!
PIGS #1 & #2:	Huh?
PIG #3:	Metal.
PIGS #1 & #2:	Oh.
PIG #3:	And cement.
PIG #1:	Cool.
MAMA PIG:	That's my boy!
PIG #2:	That's better than licorice.
PIG #3:	No kidding.
NARRATOR:	And up came the wolf.
WOLF:	I'm Big!—
NARRATOR:	—Oh, boy.
WOLF:	I'm Bad!—
NARRATOR:	—Oh, great.
WOLF:	I'm Mr. *(slowly and with feeling)* Unbelievable!
NARRATOR:	Yeah, yeah, whatever.
WOLF:	Little oinkers! Little oinkers! Let me in!
PIG #3:	No way, dude!
WOLF:	Then I'll huff and I'll puff and I'll bring you DEATH, 'Cause I got the world's worst morning BREATH!

(The three pigs pull out clothespins and put them on their noses.)

PIG #3:	Go for it, dude.
NARRATOR:	So he huffed and he puffed. But he couldn't knock down the house.
WOLF:	Bummer.
ALL PIGS:	Cool.
NARRATOR:	And so the three pigs lived happily ever after because they learned to put their mother's words into practice.
MAMA PIG:	What good little oinkers they are. I'm so proud.
EVERYONE:	The end.

(Bow. Fade out the stage lights. Exit.)

When the story is done, say, **"Do you know what Bible story that's like? Jesus once told a story about a wise man who built his house out of . . .** (quickly) **superior grade, high alloy, drop-forged, non-oriented, silicon, fully processed steel with reinforced, rebar support beams and a high-level, load-bearing-capacity concrete base . . . OK, not quite. But he did build his house on a rock. Let's look at Jesus' story and try to figure out what that house and that rock represent!"**

Then retell (see the creative ideas listed below) or read "The Wise and Foolish Builders."

Preteens can think a little more abstractly. They'll enjoy the process of seeing the connections between stories you tell about their world and the stories Jesus told about his. One way to do this is through contemporary stories that teach the same lesson as the Bible story. You could (1) **make up a story of your own** based on one of the following ideas, (2) **use these ideas as discussion starters**, or (3) **let the students role-play** what might happen if:

Quick Tip #9 - Take It for a Test-Drive!
Before telling your story to your audience, test-drive it for a while. If you were thinking of buying a car, you'd probably try it out under different road conditions to see how it handles, how it responds to you, and how well you like driving it. Well, do the same thing before taking your story off the lot! Hop in and drive it around! Test it out under different conditions. Get used to it, and make sure you know how it handles before driving it out in front of everyone else!

- Two airplane pilots both know what the instruction manual says about how to land, but only one of them decides to follow it. What happens to them?
- Two kids know all the right secret codes for winning at their favorite video game. One kid decides he doesn't need them. The other kid relies on the codes. Who wins? Why?
- Two people know the rules for soccer, but only one of them follows the rules. What happens to them both?
- Two people get bitten by a rare, deadly snake. Both of them have the antivenin in their backpacks. Both know first aid. But only one guy actually takes the medicine. What happens to the other one? Act it out very dramatically. Pretend one of you is the Crocodile Guy from TV!
- Pretend you're there at the time of Jesus' story. The storm has just finished. The two builders are trying to explain to the insurance guy what happened. What do they say?

W. E.G.I. (Weird & Extremely Goofy Ideas)

Demonstrate the difference between standing on a rock and standing on something that won't support your weight. Bring a concrete block and a giant bowl of gelatin into your classroom. Then, invite two students up front who won't mind getting their feet a little messy . . . Yup! Have 'em take off their shoes and socks and then have one of them stand in the gelatin while the other stands on the rock. Everyone will get the picture!

"The Wise and Foolish Builders" could be retold in so many creative ways! You could tell it as a **call and response** story (in which the audience all responds by saying something whenever you cue them during the story). For example, you might teach your preteens the following refrain: *"He knew it! He knew it! But the dude wouldn't do it!"* (to emphasize that the guy knew what kind of foundation to use, but didn't use it). Then, as your retell the story, cue the students when to say their part.

You could also have your students come up with a way of retelling the story from the houses' perspectives and present it as a **tandem monologue** (in which two people present monologues by alternating speaking parts). For example, the two types of ground, Rocky and Sandra, might retell the story. Sandra might say things like: "Any minute someone else will come along and build on me because it's too much work building on that rock over there. I'm not worried—I won't be alone for long!"

You could also tell this story as either a **narrative pantomime** (in which one person reads a story while others act it out) or as a **group refrain** story (in which different groups of students join along saying or doing something at specific places in a story). Both of these techniques work well with larger groups. The following version of the story combines both of these creative storytelling techniques.

Rocks and Sand!
(a narrative pantomime/group refrain version of "The Wise and Foolish Builders")

Notes for the storyteller: For the **group refrain** portion of this story, divide the audience into two groups. Tell one group they'll be the Hard Rockers. As they pound their fists into their hands, they say (with rhythm):

Rock! Rock! Built upon the rock!
Built upon the strong and sturdy rock!

The other half of the audience is the Beach Bums. All they want to do is hang out on the sand. Their part goes:

Sand! Sand! Shifting sand!
Crumbling, tumbling on the land!

Or, if you're telling the story to preteens, you might wish to use the following refrain and have the students say it in their best spooky-sounding voice: **"The sands . . . the sands . . . the shifty wifty sa-a-a-a-nds."**

Explain that they'll say their part whenever you point to them and say their cue word: Rock or Sand. Practice once or twice before beginning.

For the **narrative pantomime** portion of this story, invite 9 people up front. (Use silly costumes if you like!): Wise Builder, Foolish Builder, Wise Guy's House, Foolish Guy's House, Wind, Rain, Rock, Sand, Streams.

Explain that they'll be acting out the story as you read it. Encourage them to enjoy themselves and ham it up a little bit! Position the Builders, the Sand, and the Rock on the right side of the stage, both Houses on the left side of the stage, the Wind and Rain behind the audience, and the Streams on the floor on the right side of the stage.

Tell them to return to their position every time you say, "POSITIONS!" When the Builders build, they shape the Houses as if they were human clay!

If desired, give the Rain a watering can full of water to help with his part, and give the Streams a loaded squirt gun!

Sit in the front row of the audience as you read or tell the story. Make sure you pause long enough for everyone to do his or her actions! (Suggested comments and banter appear in bold italics. Stage directions and storytelling tips appear in italics.)

Jesus said . . . "Everyone who hears my words and puts them into practice is like a W<small>ISE</small> M<small>AN</small> . . . *step forward M<small>R</small>. W<small>ISE</small> G<small>UY</small>! . . . tap your head and look as smart as you can* . . . who built his H<small>OUSE</small> . . . *go on, build up your H<small>OUSE</small>, yeah it's over there, you gotta go get it* . . . on the R<small>OCK</small> . . .

(say this refrain with the Hard Rockers)
Rock! Rock! Built upon the rock!
Built upon the strong and sturdy rock!

Yeah, stick your H<small>OUSE</small> on it . . . go ahead! . . . The R<small>AIN</small> came down . . . *where are you, R<small>AIN</small>? Come on forward. Show us some rain* . . . the S<small>TREAMS</small> rose . . . *rise from the ground, S<small>TREAMS</small>! Rise!* . . . and the W<small>INDS</small> blew . . . *go on, blow on the H<small>OUSE</small>* . . . and beat against that H<small>OUSE</small> . . . *I said 'beat against that H<small>OUSE</small>', not 'beat up that H<small>OUSE</small>!'* . . . yet it did not fall, because it had its foundation on the R<small>OCK</small> . . ."

(say this refrain with the Hard Rockers)
Rock! Rock! Built upon the rock!
Built upon the strong and sturdy rock!

<u>POSITIONS!</u> . . . *(wait long enough for everyone to get back to their starting positions)* . . . **But everyone who hears Jesus' words and does not put them into practice is like a** F<small>OOLISH</small> M<small>AN</small> . . . *that's you* . . . who built his H<small>OUSE</small> . . . *you got it . . . go build your H<small>OUSE</small>* . . . on the S<small>AND</small> . . .

(Say the refrain with the Beach Bums. Use whichever refrain you chose. For example:)
Sand! Sand! Shifting sand!
Crumbling, tumbling on the land!

The R<small>AIN</small> came down . . . *you know the routine by now* . . . the S<small>TREAMS</small> rose . . . and the W<small>IND</small> blew . . . and beat against that H<small>OUSE</small> . . . *Sometimes they tickled it* . . . and it fell with a great crash . . . *Ouch. That's gotta hurt . . . That was a great crash all right* . . . Because it had only been built on the S<small>AND</small> . . .

(say the refrain with the Beach Bums)
Sand! Sand! Shifting sand!
Crumbling, tumbling on the land!

<u>POSITIONS!</u> . . . **By putting Jesus' words into practice in your life, you can be like the** W<small>ISE</small> M<small>AN</small> . . . *tap your brain and flex your muscles, M<small>R</small>. W<small>ISE</small> G<small>UY</small>* . . . who built his house on the R<small>OCK</small> . . .

(say the refrain with the Hard Rockers)
Rock! Rock! Built upon the rock!
Built upon the strong and sturdy rock!

And not like the F<small>OOLISH</small> M<small>AN</small> . . . *look stupid, M<small>R</small>. F<small>OOLISH</small> M<small>AN</small> . . . Oh! you're good at that* . . . who built his house on the S<small>AND</small> . . .

(say the refrain with the Beach Bums)
Sand! Sand! Shifting sand!
Crumbling, tumbling on the land!

. . . whenever the storms of life surround you! . . . Alright! Give all our volunteers a great big hand!

Finally, here's one last creative idea for this story. Teach the children the chorus to the following **song**. Wear an eye patch and sing like a Scottish sailor or a pirate!

Hey, Ho! Blow the House Down
(sing to the tune of "Blow the Man Down")

I'm go-ing to sing of two men from the land,
Hey, ho! Blow the house down!
[Oh,] one built on rock and the other on sand . . .
Give me some time to blow the house down!

There once lived two fellows—one foolish, one wise,
Hey, ho! Blow the house down!
They built their homes out on the beach near St. Ives.
Give me some time to blow the house down!

The storms and the waves came a-crashing in then,
Hey, ho! Blow the house down!
The house built on rock didn't topple or bend!
Give me some time to blow the house down!

But the house on the sand fell upon the guy's head.
Hey, ho! Blow the house down!
He should have constructed on boulders instead!
Give me some time to blow the house down!

So all those who hear but don't do what God said,
Hey, ho! Blow the house down!
Are stupid and foolish and thick in the head!
Give me some time to blow the house down!

ADDITIONAL IDEAS AND LESSON CONNECTIONS:

Build two towers: one out of sugar cubes and one out of Lego® building blocks. Then, place a little plastic house, or another item to represent the house on each tower. Pour water over them and watch the sugar cubes dissolve. (Practice this at home before doing it in front of the class so you get an idea of how long it will take for the sugar cubes to melt!) Or use coffee for the rain . . . tell the kids there was acid rain or something . . .

Or, perhaps, invite the children to build two block towers, one of them on a blanket and the other one on the floor (or carpet). Then, demonstrate what happens to the tower when you pull out the blanket . . . Look up 1 Corinthians 3:10, 11 and talk about what foundation we're building our lives on.

Talk about how Jesus doesn't want our lives to crumble. Discuss different types of "storms" of life. Then close by praying for God's help in being a doer of the Word.

For a craft idea, fill decorative baby food jars (or preserve jars) with sands of different colors and place a rock on top of the sand. The students can write a Bible verse from the story on a sheet of paper, decorate it, and then attach it to the jar.

PRAYER CONNECTION:

1. Pray for the wisdom to understand and accept God's Word.
2. Pray for the guts to put God's Word into practice.
3. Pray for the conviction to do things God's way rather than your own.

INTERACTIVE PRAYER IDEA:

Build towers out of blocks, and as each person adds her block, she adds her words to the prayer. Handing out small rocks as reminders to build our lives on Jesus' words will also help the lesson stick!

The Sower and the Four Soils 2

BASED ON: Matthew 13:1-9, 18-23; Mark 4:1-20; Luke 8:4-15

BIG IDEA: Not everyone who hears the Word of God will accept it. The condition of our hearts and the receptivity of our souls affect how we receive the gospel.

GRACE CONNECTION: God's Word will have a powerful, life-transforming result when we understand it, accept it, and believe it. God wants to bear great fruit both in our lives and through our lives as we spread his Word:

> *As the rain and the snow come down from heaven, and do not return*
> *to it without watering the earth and making it bud and flourish, so that*
> *it yields seed for the sower and bread for the eater, so is my word that*
> *goes out from my mouth: It will not return to me empty, but will*
> *accomplish what I desire and achieve the purpose for which I sent it.*
>
> *(Isaiah 55:10, 11)*

TOPICS: Distractions, faith, God's kingdom, materialism, persecution, perseverance, witnessing

MEMORY SPARKS: To find yourself in this story, think of a time when . . .
1. Interest in the things of this world choked out your interest in spiritual things . . .
2. A nugget of truth was planted in your heart, and then it was snatched away . . .
3. Something distracted you from growing in your faith . . .

To help your students connect with this story, say, "Think of a time when . . ."
1. You didn't want to go to church because you wanted to play video games or sports instead . . .
2. You lost your joy when trouble or hard times came . . .
3. You tried telling someone about Jesus, but the words didn't seem to take root in her life . . .

HERE'S WHAT'S GOING ON:

Early in his preaching ministry, Jesus used a number of parables to get people thinking about the kingdom of Heaven. (Matthew records eight parables in chapter 13 alone!)

Even though Jesus often explained his stories to his followers (see Mark 4:34), we don't have a record of many of those explanations. This is one of the few stories for which we do have an explanation.

Jesus told this story from a boat to a crowd of people who had gathered on the beach. Then later, when he was alone with his followers, he explained the meaning of the story to them. So there are actually two different settings for this story—one for its telling and one for its explanation. There are also two different audiences—the crowd (for the story) and the disciples (for the explanation).

HERE'S WHAT THE STORY'S ABOUT:

Three of the four Gospel writers record this story. Each of them retells it slightly differently, so be sure to read all three accounts before telling the story. For example, they each emphasize something different about the good soil: Matthew emphasizes **understanding the Word** (knowledge), Mark emphasizes **accepting the Word** (faith), and Luke emphasizes **retaining the Word** (perseverance).

Jesus used this story to teach about the receptivity of our hearts to the gospel message and the different dangers for which we should be on the lookout.

In the story, a farmer tossed his seed into a field, but only a small percentage of the seed produced a crop.

When the disciples got Jesus alone onshore, they told him they didn't understand his story. Jesus seemed agitated by their response: *"Don't you understand this parable? How then will you understand any parable?" (Mark 4:13).*

Jesus then explained that the seeds represent the good news of the kingdom, and the different types of soils represent different ways that people respond to the Word.

Jesus' point is that many things may distract, divert, or diminish the effect of God's Word in our lives: times of trouble and testing (persecution), spiritual adversaries (the devil), the lure of wealth (materialism), the worries of life (worry), the pursuit of pleasure (hedonism), and the insatiable desire for more (greed). Only when we hear, understand, and accept God's Word, and persevere through trials, will we produce a crop.

P.S. I've named this parable "The Sower and the Four Soils." To see the name Jesus gave the parable, flip to Matthew 13:18!

QuickTip #10 - Dusting Off Your Memories

Here are three tips for telling personal stories:

1. **Give it time.** Let the memory walk with you until you're emotionally distant enough from it to share it without being overcome by it.
2. **Step out of the spotlight.** When you tell personal stories, always be the mistake-maker rather than the hero.
3. **Make the connection.** Include people and places your listeners will be able to picture and relate to. If you can't see the story, your audience probably can't either.

TELLING THIS STORY TO STUDENTS AGES 3-7

Even young children can sit and listen to a short story like this one. When you tell this story, consider pulling your props out of a **story bag**. Choose a colorful cloth bag (or use a vest with lots of pockets). Then, place a farmer's hat, seeds, a rock, a small plush bird toy, some thorns (buy a rose on the way to class), a flashlight (to represent the sun), and some dark, rich soil (or a picture of a farmer's field) inside the bag. You may even wish to provide packets of seeds for the students to take home with them.

As you tell the story, pull out the items that relate to the events or images in the story. (Cue words are underlined.) Then set them on a table up front (if you have a large group) or on the floor in front of your class (if you have a small group).

By using a story bag, you allow the natural curiosity of the students to work to your advantage. They'll be sure to pay attention because they'll want to know what you're going to pull out next!

One day, a <u>farmer</u> *(pull out the farmer's hat and put it on)* **went out to plant some <u>seeds.</u>** *(pull out the seeds)*

He threw some of the seeds on the path, but the <u>birds</u> came *(pull out the bird)* and <u>ate them up</u>! *(make your toy bird eat up the seeds)*

He threw some of the seeds in the <u>rocky soil</u>. *(pull out the rock)* At first the plants grew up quickly, but soon the <u>sun</u> came out. *(pull out the flashlight, shine it at your students and at the rock)* And the plants <u>dried up and died</u> *(make the sound of dying plants, "Ahhh!")* because they didn't have deep roots.

Some seeds fell among the <u>thorny plants</u>. *(pull out the thorns or rose)* **But as the seeds grew, <u>the thorny plants choked them out</u>!** *(make your thorns attack the seeds)*

Some seeds fell on <u>good soil</u>. *(If you're using soil, pull it out and talk to it soothingly: "Good soil! That's a good soil! . . .")* **They grew strong and healthy and <u>produced even more plants</u> than there were at the start!** *(if you're using a picture of a farmer's field, pull it out)*

The end. *(put your items away for later)*

> ## QuickTip #11 - Don't Drop Your Props!
> When using props, remember to use things that you can manipulate easily and that won't become a distraction to your listeners. Also be sure to use items that are large enough to be seen by everyone in the room.
>
> Rather than using small props that might be hard to see (such as seeds), make them bigger! Use basketballs, balloons, or even beach balls for the seeds! Always look for ways to make the story more visual, engaging, and easier to remember.
>
> Use your imagination and come up with fun, memorable props of your own to add to the stories you tell!

Once you've told this parable, you may wish to have the students participate in a creative dramatics activity based on the story. Listed below is an example of a **story dramatization** version of the parable.

Poof! You're a Seed!
(a story dramatization of "The Sower and the Four Soils")

Notes for the storyteller: Listed below is a sample text of what you might say to your students. Practice it a few times before class, but don't try to memorize it. When it comes time to actually tell the story, lead this activity in your own way and in your own words. Be sure to pause long enough to give the students a chance to do the actions!

OK, kids, let's pretend that we're becoming the different things in this story! It'll be fun! First of all, let's all pretend to be the <u>farmer</u>! . . . Walk like a farmer . . . He's carrying a big bag of seeds! Lift up your bag of seeds and show me how heavy it is! Great job . . . Now, let's toss our seeds out into the field . . . Throw lots of seeds out there because we want to grow lots of plants! . . . More seeds! . . . More! . . . And more! . . . Good! . . .

Now, let's pretend that we're those <u>seeds</u>, growing in the ground . . . You're no longer a farmer. Everybody get small! Scrunch up like a seed . . . 1-2-3 POOF! YOU'RE A SEED!

Now, here comes the water from the rain . . . Drink it in . . . Ahhh! . . . and now you're growing . . . and growing . . . and growing . . . good! Feel that warm sunlight! . . . Ahhh! . . . Put on some suntan lotion . . . Very nice . . . Grow really big now! . . . Watch out, 'cause here come the birds! . . . Ready, let's all change into the <u>birds</u>! 1-2-3 POOF! YOU'RE A BIRD!

Fly around the room a little bit, but don't bump into anyone! OK, now pretend that you're eating up little plants off the ground . . . Yummy! . . . Get ready to change into something else, because now we're gonna turn into some mean, prickly <u>thorns</u> . . . Ready . . . 1-2-3 POOF! YOU'RE A THORNBUSH!

Show me how pointy your thorns are! Show me a mean, prickly, thorny face! Ooh . . . We have some scary thornbushes in here! . . . OK, now pretend that some little baby plants are trying to grow up near you and you don't want 'em there—try to scare 'em away when I count to three! Ready? 1-2-3! . . . Wow! No plants will wanna grow near you! Next, we're gonna become <u>rocks</u>. Ready? 1-2-3 POOF! YOU'RE A ROCK!

Rocks don't move. They're frozen. They're stiff. They're strong. Even if you tickle a rock, it won't laugh . . . Let's see if we have some rocks in here that won't laugh even if I tickle 'em . . . *(if desired, tickle a couple of students on the tummy)* . . . Good rocks! . . . Next, we're all gonna turn into something that dries out the plants growing up near the rocks. Ready to turn into the <u>sun</u>? Here we go! 1-2-3 POOF! YOU'RE THE SUN!

Shine bright! Float across the sky! . . . Whee! . . . Show me how bright you can shine . . . Good job! Finally, we're gonna turn back into <u>seeds</u> again. But this time, when we land in good soil, no thorns or birds or sun can hurt us . . . Ready? We're gonna grow into super tall plants! Let's see who can be the tallest plant of all! Ready? 1-2-3 POOF! YOU'RE A GROWING PLANT!

Good job! The <u>good soil</u> in this story is like a person who wants to follow Jesus! His heart is close to God, and lots of good things come out of his life. Let's all say together, "I want to follow Jesus!" Ready? 1-2-3, "I WANT TO FOLLOW JESUS!" Good job!

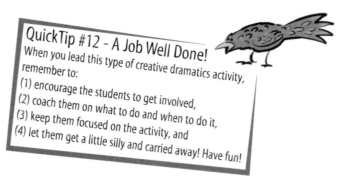

QuickTip #12 - A Job Well Done!
When you lead this type of creative dramatics activity, remember to:
(1) encourage the students to get involved,
(2) coach them on what to do and when to do it,
(3) keep them focused on the activity, and
(4) let them get a little silly and carried away! Have fun!

When you're done telling or acting out this story, you'll want to help your students understand that the different items in the story represent different things in real life. Say something like:

God wants your faith to grow, just like a seed grows in the ground. But there are some bad things that might try to stop your love of God from growing! Jesus explained that the farmer *(pull out the farmer's hat again and hold it up)* is like a man who tells other people about Jesus. In this class, that's me!

The seeds *(hold up the seeds)* are all the stories I tell you about Jesus. Are they going into your heart? I hope so!

If someone hears about Jesus but doesn't understand, then it's like a bird coming *(hold up the birds)* and snatching God's Word from his heart! We don't want that to happen!

If someone hears about Jesus but doesn't grow stronger in her faith—or if she stops loving him when hard times come—*(hold up the flashlight)* it's like the plants that dried out in the hot sun. We don't want that to happen either!

People who get too worried about making lots of money and forget about following Jesus are like the plants that got choked out by the thorns. *(hold up the rose or thorns)* So let's all keep away from greed! That can hurt our love for God!

But those who hear God's Word, believe it, and live it out, are like the seeds that fell on good soil. *(if you are using soil, hold it up)* They made more and more seeds grow!

Let's all pray that we grow a healthy faith and grow closer to Jesus by hearing, understanding, and believing in God's Word! *(if you're using a picture of a farmer's field, pull it out)*

The end.

Old MacDonald

(to the tune of Old MacDonald)

Old MacDonald had a farm, E-I-E-I-O!
And on this farm he <u>planted seeds</u>. E-I-E-I-O!
With *(jump up and down)* some popcorn here . . .
and some popcorn there . . .
Here a pop . . . There a pop . . . Everywhere [some] popcorn . . .
Old MacDonald had a farm, E-I-E-I-O!

And on this farm he had some <u>birds</u>. E-I-E-I-O!
With a *(flap your wings)* "Caw! Caw!" here . . .
and a "Caw! Caw!" there . . .
Here a "Caw!" . . . There a "Caw!" . . . Everywhere a "Caw! Caw!" . . .
Old MacDonald had a farm, E-I-E-I-O!

And on this farm he had some <u>rocks</u>. E-I-E-I-O!
With a *(playing an air guitar, singing in your best British rock star voice)*
"Rock! Rock!" here . . . and a "Rock! Rock!" there . . .
Here a "Rock!" . . . There a "Rock!" . . . Everywhere a "Rock! Rock!" . . .
Old MacDonald had a farm, E-I-E-I-O!

And on this farm he had some <u>thorns</u>. E-I-E-I-O!
With a *(poke someone close by)* "Poke! Poke!" here . . .
and a "Poke! Poke!" there . . .
Here a "Poke!" . . . There a "Poke!" . . . Everywhere a "Poke! Poke!" . . .
Old MacDonald had a farm, E-I-E-I-O!

And on this farm he had <u>good soil</u>. E-I-E-I-O!
With *(raise your hands high)* a big crop here . . .
and a big crop there . . .
Here a crop . . . There a crop . . . Everywhere a big crop . . .
Old MacDonald had a farm, E-I-E-I-O!

		Creative Connection Section
Field Trip Ideas		Matthew 13:1-3 mentions that Jesus told this story from a boat to a large crowd of people who'd gathered on the shore. If your church is near a lake, consider retelling this story from a boat near the shore like Jesus did!
Mood and Atmosphere		Thought-provoking, reflective . . .
Sensory Connections	Sight	Put shovels, trowels, picks, hoes, or other farm implements around your classroom to create the atmosphere of working on a farm.
	Touch	Place four types of soil: (1) rocky, (2) sandy, (3) packed, and (4) moist into jars or shoe boxes. Then, hold up a dark sheet to block the view of the children as they feel the different types of soil. Have them guess which soil from the story each one represents! As you tell the story, hand out the props. Maybe even pull them out of a wheelbarrow!
	Hearing	Consider having the children make sound effects for the blowing wind, cawing birds, angry thorns, sizzling sun, and happy farmer.
	Taste	Have popcorn for a snack and talk about how corn grows in a field, and each stalk of corn that grows produces more and more kernels of corn. Popcorn starts small and it pops big, just like the seeds in good soil!
	Smell	Gather things that grow in soil such as flowers, pinecones, or various fruits and vegetables. Let the children touch, smell, or (if applicable) eat them for a snack. Then talk about how God wants to grow fruit in our lives too! (See Galatians 5:22, 23.)
Costume Ideas		Overalls, boots, and a pitchfork.

TELLING THIS STORY TO STUDENTS AGES 8-12

Since there's a lot of action in this story, it would be an easy story for your students to act out. With older students, don't tell the story first, but rather invite the students to act out the story as you read or tell it. This teaching technique is called **narrative pantomime**.

For example: Invite 12 students up front. Assign them the following parts: 1 FARMER, 4 SEEDS, 1 SUN, 2 ROCKS, 2 THORNS, 2 BIRDS.

Have the BIRDS start in the back of the room, behind the listeners. Position the FARMER and the SEEDS on the left side of the stage, the ROCKS in the center, and the THORNS on the right. If desired, allow your students to wear crazy costumes.

After assigning the parts, go and sit in the front row of the audience and read or tell the story. Pause long enough for everyone to do the actions. Prompt them on what to do next if they're unsure. And then, respond to whatever happens onstage, using it to move the story forward!

When you look for a way to retell a parable like this to preteens, look for parallels in our world. The farmer sent out lots of seeds, but the seeds encountered different problems, and only a few of them grew. After summarizing the story, translate it into the language of today for a **contemporary retelling**. For example, you could retell this story as a surfer dude from the beach!

The Parable of the Surfer
(a contemporary retelling of "The Sower and the Four Soils")

Notes for the storyteller: When you tell this story, grab a surfboard and cool sunglasses, dress up like a surfer, and remember to totally talk like a surfer, dude!

So there was this dude, you know? And he like found out from The Weather Channel there were gonna be awesome waves the next day in Montego Bay. So he was like, "This SO rocks!"

And so the dude e-mailed all his surfer friends and he was like, "Dudes, meet me at the beach tomorrow. And don't forget your boards!"

But some of the other surfer dudes, they never even showed up because they thought he said, "Meet me at the leech!" And they were like, "Dude, I don't like leeches (optional, "they suck . . ."). **So I think they went to Wal-Mart® instead.**

And some of 'em drove to the beach and dove into the waves, but since they weren't like too experienced or anything, the waves totally washed away their swimsuits. Bummer. So they went home . . . naked!

And some of 'em were like, "Awesome!" And they started drivin' to the beach, but then they stopped at this gas station to buy some cheese curls and beef jerky. And they got so distracted playin' video games that they never even made it to the water's edge.

But some dudes grabbed their surfboards and caught a wave and totally had an awesome time! And they were all like, "This SO rocks!"

(The explanation to the story is found below.)

And so, in the story, the Surfer Dude is like the youth pastor 'cause he's got a goatee and everything . . . and the e-mail is like the Bible, even though it would be too long to e-mail anyway, even if you sent it as an attached file . . .

And the dudes who didn't understand it are like the people who totally don't get the Bible . . . and the dudes who got distracted are like the dudes who . . . get distracted—what's that over there! . . . *(point to the wall behind the students)* **gotcha . . .**

And the dudes who lost their suits and were naked and everything are the people who give up on God . . . I don't really get that one either . . .

And the dudes who surfed all day in the hot, hot sun were like, well, I think you can guess who they're like, my friendly dudes and dudettes.

And the surfing, well, that's totally like the kingdom of God. I guess 'cause Jesus invented surfin' and he didn't even need a surfboard!

God rocks!

To help your students make the connection between the events in the story and what they represent in real life, you may wish to play a Human Matching **Game**. Make 12 signs, one for each of the following items:

STORY REFERENCES:	WHAT THEY REPRESENT:
sign #1 - Trampled Soil	sign #5 - I don't get it!
sign #3 - Rocky Soil	sign #8 - I forget it!
sign #6 - Thorny Soil	sign #12 - I quit it!
sign #10 - Good Soil	sign #11- I get it!
sign #9 - Farmer	sign #2 - I transmit it!
sign #4 - Seeds	sign #7 - I'm the Word! I admit it!

Give the signs to 12 children. Then have your students see if they can match up which 2 people go together. Invite a student onstage and see how quickly he or she can match up all 6 pairs. If you have a large group, try the game once with all boys and once with all girls. See who's faster, the brotherhood or the sisterhood!

W.E.G.I. (Weird & Extremely Goofy Ideas)

In lots of video games, students are able to shoot lasers repeatedly at alien invaders, but only hit them occasionally because the targets are moving or are hiding behind obstructions.

This is similar to the farmer scattering his seeds and only having a small percentage of them "hit the mark"! Consider playing a video game to help relate this story to the world of your preteen listeners!

PRAYER CONNECTION:

1. Pray for people who spread God's Word, that they remain faithful and bold in telling people about Jesus.
2. Pray for those who hear God's Word, that they would understand it, believe it, and produce a crop.
3. Pray for people who are facing thorns, that God would help them to persevere through the tough times.

INTERACTIVE PRAYER IDEA:

Hand out packets of seeds to the children. Hold up the packets as you pray for different people by name, asking that God's Word would take root in their hearts.

The Unmerciful Servant

BASED ON: Matthew 18:21-35

BIG IDEA: We should forgive others from the heart as freely and as often as God forgives us.

GOSPEL CONNECTION: God's forgiveness is full, free, and forever. It should change the way we relate to others. We need to be quick to forgive others, just as God is quick to forgive us:

> *Bear with each other and forgive whatever grievances you may have against one another. Forgive as the Lord forgave you. (Colossians 3:13)*

TOPICS: Consequences, forgiveness, God's kingdom, grace, grudges, judgment, mercy, unforgiveness

MEMORY SPARKS: To find yourself in this story, think of a time when . . .
1. You didn't feel like forgiving someone . . . What happened?
2. You treated someone with justice, but without mercy . . .
3. Someone forgave you, but it didn't change your life
   (even though it should have) . . .

To help your students connect with this story, say, "Think of a time when . . ."
1. You held a grudge against someone . . . What happened? Did it help or hurt?
2. You were more concerned about being fair than about showing mercy . . .
3. You did something wrong and someone forgave you . . . How did that make you feel?

HERE'S WHAT'S GOING ON:

In the wake of Jesus' teachings about forgiveness, Peter asked Jesus if he should forgive people up to 7 times. Many Jews considered 3 times a generous number of times to forgive, so Peter wasn't skimping when he suggested 7 times.

Well, Jesus said that 77 times would be more on target! Jesus' point wasn't that we should keep a tally of the wrongs of others, but that we should forgive others unconditionally and without reservation because that's how God has forgiven us.

Then, to further emphasize his point, Jesus told Peter (and us!) this story.

HERE'S WHAT THE STORY'S ABOUT:

In this well-known story, a man is forgiven a debt of millions of dollars but refuses to be merciful to someone who owes him only a few bucks. As a result, the king who canceled the man's debt changes his mind and sends him off to be tortured instead.

> *In anger his master turned him over to the jailers to be tortured, until he should pay back all he owed. This is how my heavenly Father will treat each of you unless you forgive your brother from your heart.*   (Matthew 18:34, 35)

Yes, Jesus actually said that those of us who refuse to forgive others will be tortured.

Now was he just exaggerating to make a point? Maybe using hyperbole or another figure of speech? Well, I think we should take him at his word. But however you interpret Jesus' summary of his story, his point is crystal clear—forgive others from your heart or you'll regret it. If we're

unwilling to forgive others, we shouldn't expect God to forgive us. As Jesus put it on a different occasion:

> *For if you forgive men when they sin against you, your heavenly Father will*
> *also forgive you. But if you do not forgive men their sins, your Father will not forgive*
> *your sins.*   *(Matthew 6:14, 15)*

So, while it's true that this story does show a picture of God's gracious forgiveness to us, the main point of the story is that we need to graciously forgive other people.

> **QuickTip #13 - The Fun Factor!**
> Whatever creative storytelling ideas you decide to use, make the lesson fun and interactive for your students. Remember, if kids aren't having fun, they're probably not learning!

TELLING THIS STORY TO STUDENTS AGES 3-7

A great way to involve students is through a **masks** story. Whenever you say the cue word, the listeners put on imaginary masks and then take them off right away.

The Man Who Refused to Forgive
(a masks version of "The Unmerciful Servant")

Notes for the storytellers: In this story there are 4 masks: happy, sad, surprised, and angry. (I've added an extra one too, just for fun!)

Options - You may wish to tell the story yourself and have another storyteller (or storytellers) lead the putting on and taking off of the imaginary masks. (Cue words are underlined.) You could even hold up cue cards to let the listeners know when to put on their masks.

The speaking parts are split up to make it easier for you if you choose to use two storytellers.

BONNIE: One day, Peter came to Jesus and asked how many times he should forgive people. "Is 7 times enough?" he asked.

GEORGE: But Jesus said, "Not 7 times times, but 77 times!" And when he said that, Peter was <u>surprised</u>!

BONNIE: And then, Jesus told him this story . . .

GEORGE: Once, there was a servant who owed the king lots of money. In fact, he owed him millions of dollars! And whenever the king let him borrow more money, he was <u>happy</u>!

BONNIE: So when the king told him he had to pay it all back, he was <u>sad</u>. And he said,

GEORGE: (as the servant) "I can't pay you back. I've used it all up buying candy bars!"

BONNIE: Well, something like that . . . And then, the king got <u>angry</u>!

GEORGE: (as the king) "Then you and your children and your wife are all gonna be sold as slaves until you can pay your debt!" When the servant heard that, he was <u>surprised</u>.

BONNIE: And <u>sad</u> . . . He dropped to his knees and said, "Oh, please! Give me more time! I'll pay it all back! I promise!"

GEORGE: Well, the king thought about it and decided to cancel that servant's debt and let him go. When the servant thought about it, he was very, very, very <u>surprised</u>!

BONNIE: And <u>happy</u>! . . . But then, something unexpected happened. That servant went out and found someone who owed him a couple of dollars. And he got <u>angry</u>.

GEORGE: *(as the servant)* "Pay me my money! I want more candy bars!"

BONNIE: And, he started choking the guy! When he did that, the poor guy was really <u>surprised</u>!

GEORGE: And he was choking! *(make up a mask for this)*

BONNIE: But then the man dropped to his knees and said, "Oh, please! Give me more time! I'll pay it all back! I promise!" Just like the other guy had done.

GEORGE: But instead of canceling the man's debt, he sent him to prison until he could pay the money! And that made the guy really <u>sad</u>.

BONNIE: When he did that, the other servants were <u>surprised</u>!

GEORGE: They went to tell the king, and when the king heard about all that, he got really <u>angry</u>!

BONNIE: So, once again, he called in the servant who had owed him all that money.

GEORGE: *(as the king)* "You wicked man! I canceled your debt, but you refused to have mercy on this other guy!"

BONNIE: When the servant found out the king knew about what he'd done, he was <u>surprised</u>.

GEORGE: And <u>sad</u>—

BONNIE: —because the king was <u>angry</u>—

GEORGE: —and not very <u>happy</u>!

BONNIE: So the king sent him to jail where people would hit him!

GEORGE: And believe me, that guy was very <u>sad</u>.

BONNIE: And then, Jesus said, "That's how God will treat you unless you forgive others from your heart."

GEORGE: 'Cause when we hold a grudge and refuse to forgive It makes the Lord <u>angry</u> . . . at the way that we live!

BONNIE: But when we forgive others, God's <u>happy</u> . . . because Then we're treating others like he's treated us!

TOGETHER: The end!

(Bow. Fade out the stage lights. Exit.)

When the story is over, discuss why it's so hard to forgive other people, and why it's so important to God that we do! Say something like, **"Do you really think Jesus wants us to keep track of how many times we forgive someone? If not, then what did he mean when he said we should forgive a person 77 times? . . . That's right! Jesus wants us to forgive ALL THE TIME, just like God does."**

Fish Tales with Uncle Lenny

Here's a fun way to include a natural storyteller from your church into your children's ministry. Invite a man from your congregation to become "Uncle Lenny—the Story Guy." Tell him you're only asking for 15 minutes of his time each week. Buy him a fishing vest, floppy fishing hat (with all those lures), and tackle box (if he doesn't have all that stuff already!). Then ask him to come to your Sunday school class or children's church and share a Bible story.

He can begin with a joke and then tell the story, pulling out **props** from his many pockets in the fishing vest or from within the tackle box! (Hey, we're all supposed to be fishers of men, right? And fishermen are natural storytellers!)

Here's a suggested way he could retell this story. Younger children may not understand all the corny fish puns (underlined), but they will enjoy seeing the funny stuff Uncle Lenny pulls out!

> **Kids, today's story is about a man** (pull out a Hulk* action figure) **who owed his king** (pull out a Spiderman* action figure) **lots of money.**
>
> **He owed him millions and millions of dollars!** (pull out a sand dollar) **And that's a lot of <u>mackerels</u>! . . . I mean, he'd been <u>lured</u>** (a fishing lure) **in deeper and deeper, until he was up to his <u>gills</u> in debt! . . .**
>
> **So one day the king told the guy he had to pay up.**
>
> **And the guy got scared!** (shake Hulk around)
>
> **"<u>Whale</u> you please give me more time?!" he said.**
>
> **Finally, the king agreed. He let the guy go and canceled his debt! He was so happy** (dance Hulk around) **he called up all his friends on his <u>shell</u> phone!** (hold up a cell phone)
>
> **But then, he went and found this other guy** (hold up a G.I. Joe* figure) **who owed him only a few dollars.** (hold up the sand dollar)
>
> **"You <u>shrimp</u>!" he said. "You owe me money! Pay me now!"**
>
> **And then he started choking the guy! The poor guy started to <u>flounder</u> all over the place! He couldn't even breathe! He was <u>like a fish out of water</u>!**
>
> **The guy begged for mercy,** (make G.I. Joe beg) **but the other man said, "<u>Clam</u> up! You're going to jail until you pay me back!"**
>
> **Well, when the other servants saw that, they told the king. And the king called him back in.**
>
> **"I <u>cod</u> have made you pay me, but I forgave you! And then you go and <u>reel in</u> this other guy and send him to jail! That's it! You're going to jail, and I'm gonna let the guards hit you until you pay me what you owe!"**
>
> **And as they took him away, the guy was yelling, "<u>Kelp</u>! <u>Kelp</u>! Somebody <u>kelp</u> me!"** (put Hulk away)
>
> **God wants us to practice <u>catch-and-release forgiveness</u>—**(hold up your fishing rod and reel)**—when we catch someone doing something wrong to us, we should release him of the wrong. Just like God does for us. And we should do it all the time, not just once in a <u>whale</u>!**
>
> **So be quick to forgive and slow to get mad.**
>
> **And it'll make Jesus happy, not sad.**
>
> **The end.**

*Incredible Hulk® is a registered trademark of Marvel Comics.
*Spiderman® is a registered trademark of Marvel Comics.
*GI Joe® is a registered trademark of Hasbro Inc.

	Creative Connection Section	
Field Trip Ideas	Tell this story in front of a bank or an ATM machine.	
Mood and Atmosphere	The story starts out happy and ends with a sad, dramatic plunge.	
Sensory Connections	**Sight**	Use silly props or dolls as described above.
	Touch	Pass around coins from other countries. Or use piles and piles of play money to help children picture the difference between $1,000,000 and a few bucks.
	Hearing	Use a gong and a flute. Whenever something goes right in the story (when someone is forgiving) play the flute; but when something goes wrong or they do something mean, hit the gong!
	Taste	Go to a vending machine and ask, "Has anyone ever lost money in one of these things?" Explain that forgiveness means to pay someone else's debts yourself! Then, buy snacks for your class!
	Smell	Bring two contrasting items—one that stinks and one that smells nice. Talk about how badly it stinks to God when we hold a grudge, but how sweet-smelling it is to forgive!
Costume Ideas	This story is great for costumes since it has three very distinct people: a king (put on a crown), a bunch of servants (wear bandannas), and some guards (carry fake swords).	

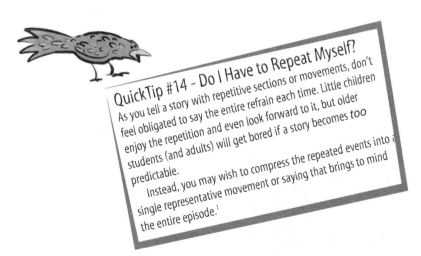

QuickTip #14 - Do I Have to Repeat Myself?
As you tell a story with repetitive sections or movements, don't feel obligated to say the entire refrain each time. Little children enjoy the repetition and even look forward to it, but older students (and adults) will get bored if a story becomes *too* predictable.
    Instead, you may wish to compress the repeated events into a single representative movement or saying that brings to mind the entire episode.[1]

---

[1] My thanks go out to storyteller David Novak, who brought this point out in a workshop of his that I attended years ago.

TELLING THIS STORY TO STUDENTS AGES 8-12

Use the following script for a **reader's theatre** presentation or a **puppet play**. You could have your students (or some teen volunteers) read the parts.

Called to Account

(a reader's theatre version of "The Unmerciful Servant")

Notes for the storytellers: You'll need 4 performers for this story: TELLER #1 (girl or boy), SERVANT (preferably a boy—you'll need a cell phone), TELLER #2 (girl or boy), KING (preferably a boy—wear a crown).

After photocopying and handing out the scripts, have each reader circle or highlight all of his speaking lines. This will help everyone know when to say their parts.

To begin this story, position the TELLERS on the left side of the stage, the SERVANTS in the center, and the KING on the right side of the stage. Bring up the stage lights, and then begin when the listeners are quiet.

TEACHER: **Lights! . . . Camera! . . . Action!**

TELLER #1: **When Peter asked Jesus how many times he should forgive someone, Jesus told him a story . . .**

TELLER #2: **Long ago there was a kind king . . .**

TELLER #1: **. . . who often lent money to the people of his kingdom.**

KING: *(smiling)* **What can I say, I'm just that kind of a guy!**

TELLER #2: **One day, he decided it was time for him to get his money back from all the people he'd lent it to.**

TELLER #1: **And there was one guy who'd borrowed millions and millions of dollars from the king.**

SERVANT: *(talking on the phone to your wife)* **Yeah, this is me! Listen, sweetie pie, I've got good news! Yeah! The king called for me! Yup. I think I'm gonna ask him for some more money. Maybe we can buy that monster truck we've been talking about . . . I know, I know I've borrowed a lot. But I'll pay him back, don't worry. OK, talk to you later. Gotta go. Bye.** *(hang up)*

TELLER #1: **So the king called him in.**

KING: **Hello.**

SERVANT: **Hey, there, kingy baby!**

KING: **Two things.**

SERVANT: **Yeah?**

KING: **Number one, don't call me kingy baby.**

SERVANT: **Oh. OK.**

KING: **Number two, I want you to pay me back all the money you owe me.**

SERVANT: **Um . . . *all* the money?**

KING: **Yup . . . You do have the money, don't you?**

SERVANT: **Well, not exactly . . . could I have a little more time . . . Please?**

KING: How much time?

SERVANT: A couple hundred years would be nice . . .

KING: Um, no. And since you can't pay what you owe me, you and your wife and your kids are gonna have to be sold as slaves until you can repay the debt.

SERVANT: Slaves?

KING: Yes. Guards, take him away!

TELLER #2: So the man did the only thing he could think to do . . .

SERVANT: Just a second, kingy bab—I mean, Mr. King Dude . . . *(talking on the phone)* Yeah, wifey baby, listen. I've got some, um, bad news. You don't mind being sold as a slave for the rest of your life to help pay back my debt, do you? . . . Honey? Are you there? Hello? *(hang up)*

TELLER #1: No, actually he didn't call his wife.

TELLER #2: But he did fall to his knees before the king . . . *(to the SERVANT)* Fall to your knees already.

SERVANT: *(falling to his knees before the KING)* Oh, please! Please! Be patient! I promise, I'll pay back everything. Pretty please with sugar on top?

TELLER #1: And the king felt bad for him and decided to cancel the whole debt.

KING: *(thoughtfully)* Hm . . . alright. I've decided to cancel the whole debt.

SERVANT: Really?

KING: Really.

SERVANT: Cool! You're the greatest, kingy baby!

KING: Don't call me kingy baby.

SERVANT: Oops.

TELLER #2: Now, you'd think that this guy would have learned to be merciful.

TELLER #1: You'd think so—

TELLER #2: —but that's not what happened.

SERVANT: *(talking on the phone)* Hey, listen, honey! Good news! Yeah, you're not gonna believe this. No, I'm not a slave yet. But the king, yeah, he canceled my debt! We don't have to be sold as slaves after all! And maybe I can still buy you that monster truck . . . Yeah, don't worry, I know how I can get the money. See you soon. Bye! *(hang up)*

TELLER #1: And, as soon as he left the palace, he found someone who owed him a few dollars.

TELLER #2: He grabbed the guy and began to choke him!

TELLER #1: *(as if choking)* Ah! Please be patient!

SERVANT: No! No! I want my money! I want to buy a monster truck!

TELLER #1: *(still choking)* I'll pay you back, I promise!

SERVANT: I want it now! *(evil laugh!)*

TELLER #2: **So, he had the guy thrown into prison until he could pay him back!**

SERVANT: *(wiping off your hands)* **That'll teach him.**

TELLER #1: **Well, when the other servants saw what had happened, they told everything to the king.**

KING: **What! But I just told him I'd cancel his debt! Bring that guy back in here!**

SERVANT: *(talking on the phone)* **Hey, honey? Yeah, it's me again! I think we'll be getting that monster truck real soon! Yeah, I found this guy who owed me some money and stuck him in prison until he can cough up the dough—oh, wait a minute, here come some of the king's guards . . . Maybe the king wants to lend me some money until next month! Yeah, talk to you soon. OK, bye.** *(hang up)*

TELLER #2: **They brought the man before the king.**

SERVANT: **Hey, kingy baby!**

KING: **You wicked man!**

SERVANT: **Yikes. You really are sensitive about the kingy baby thing, aren't you?**

KING: **I canceled your debt of millions of dollars, and you refused to have mercy on a guy who only owed you a couple of bucks!**

SERVANT: **Oh . . . you heard about that?**

KING: **Shouldn't you have had mercy on him the same way I had mercy on you?**

SERVANT: **Um . . . Is that a trick question?**

KING: **Guards! Throw this man in jail to be tortured until he can pay back the whole amount!**

SERVANT: *(to the audience)* **Tortured? Did he say "tortured"?**

KING: **Some people never learn . . .**

SERVANT: *(to the KING)* **Does this mean you're not gonna buy me that monster truck?**

TELLER #1: **And so, the guards took him away.**

SERVANT: *(to the audience)* **I want my mommy.**

TELLER #2: **And Jesus said to Peter, "That's how your heavenly Father will treat you, unless you forgive your brother from the heart."**

EVERYONE: *(together)* **The end!**

(Smile, bow, and then take your seats.)

Say something like, **"Not a very happy ending, is it? Jesus wanted this story to shake up Peter, and he wants it to shake us up too. Jesus wants the way we treat others to reflect the way God has treated us. And that means we need to forgive others willingly, freely, and often."**

You could also tell this story with **refrains** that your students can chant and perform as a round while you tell the story. Before beginning the story, divide the audience into three groups.

- GROUP 1 - Create the beat for this chant by slapping your legs and clapping your hands to this rhythm: Slap, slap. Clap, clap. Slap, slap. Clap . . . Slap, slap. Clap, clap. Slap, slap. Clap. On the slaps you say "Boom" and on the claps you say "Chicka": ***"Boom, boom, Chicka, chicka. Boom, boom. Chick! . . . Boom, boom, Chicka, chicka. Boom, boom. Chick."***

- GROUP 2 - ***"Gimme my mo-ney, baby! Gimme my dough!"*** While saying this part, wave your hands back and forth over your head.

- GROUP 3 - ***"[Oh] please show me mercy, 'cause I'll pay ya back, ya know."*** While saying this part, bop your head back and forth like an airhead.

Practice by yourself to make sure you're comfortable hearing the rhythms and weaving the refrains into a round. Explain that all groups will stop doing their parts whenever you raise both hands. Then, tell the story and add the groups one at a time, as directed below.

Once there was a guy who owed the king a lot of money. So one day, the king called him to settle his account . . .
(Start GROUP 1 to get the beat going . . . add GROUP 2 . . . end them after they've done their parts a few times)

But the guy begged for mercy . . .
(Start GROUP 1 to get the beat going . . . then add GROUP 3 . . .)

So the king forgave his huge debt of millions of dollars! And then, the first thing the guy did was find someone who owed him a few dollars, and he said . . .
(Start GROUP 1 to get the beat going . . . then add GROUP 2 . . .)

But the guy begged for mercy . . .
(Start GROUP 1 to get the beat going . . . then add GROUP 3 . . .)

Well, the man who'd been forgiven by the king didn't show any mercy. Instead, he sent the other guy to jail! So when the king heard about it, he had the man brought back in.
"You owed me millions of dollars!" he said. "But when I called you in and asked for my money, you begged for mercy!"
(Start GROUP 1 to get the beat going . . . then add GROUP 2, and then add GROUP 3 as well!)

"I showed you mercy, but you didn't show mercy to others! So now, you're gonna be the one going to jail . . . and you're gonna be tortured too!"
And Jesus ended his story by saying, "The same thing will happen to anyone who doesn't forgive others from his heart."
The end.

W.E.G.I. (Weird & Extremely Goofy Ideas)

Have the students create a movie preview of this story. Divide into groups of 3–4 students. They'll need to choose a narrator to say the voice-over part. The other students in each group reenact brief scenes from the story.

Then, take turns performing the previews. Videotape them and post the videos on your Web site. Have the students tell relatives to click on and watch!

Prayer Connection:

1. Pray for the ability to forgive and forget.
2. Ask God to forgive you for the times you've held grudges.
3. Ask the Holy Spirit to remind you how much God has forgiven you.

Interactive Prayer Idea:

Teach the children this little rhyme: ***"Jesus, here is some stuff that I've wanted to say . . . Here is a prayer that I've wanted to pray . . ."*** Repeat the refrain after each person's prayer!

The Good Samaritan

4

BASED ON: Luke 10:25-37

BIG IDEA: We need to love others by showing compassion to everyone (not just the people we'd prefer to love).

GRACE CONNECTION: God's grace is evident in his love for us and his forgiveness for us, even though we all have failed repeatedly to keep the two commands that matter most: love God and love others. God will forgive us, but we must admit our sins and quit looking for excuses and loopholes. Jesus told this story specifically to convict a man of the fact that he had not loved his neighbor as he should have.

> *If we claim to be without sin, we deceive ourselves and the truth is not in us. If we confess our sins, he is faithful and just and will forgive us our sins and purify us from all unrighteousness. If we claim we have not sinned, we make him out to be a liar and his word has no place in our lives.*   *(1 John 1:8-10)*

TOPICS: Compassion, Heaven, love, mercy, prejudice, priorities

MEMORY SPARKS: To find yourself in this story, think of a time when . . .
1. You tried to justify your behavior before God . . .
2. Someone you didn't expect showed compassion to you . . .
3. You drove by a stalled car without stopping to help . . .

To help your students connect with this story, say, "Think of a time when . . ."
1. You made fun of someone because of what she wore, where she lived, or how she looked . . .
2. You knew you should be nice to this one kid, but you decided not to be . . .
3. Instead of admitting you did something wrong, you tried to get away with it . . .

HERE'S WHAT'S GOING ON:

This is perhaps Jesus' most well-known and least understood story.

One day, a man who'd spent lots of time studying the Old Testament asked Jesus a pointed question—*"Teacher, what must I do to inherit eternal life?" (Luke 10:25).*

Jesus threw the question back into his court, asking him, in essence, "What does the Bible say? How do you interpret it?"

The man answered:

> *"Love the Lord your God with all your heart and with all your soul and with all your strength and with all your mind"; and, "Love your neighbor as yourself." "You have answered correctly," Jesus replied. "Do this and you will live."*
>
> *(Luke 10:27, 28)*

Indeed, Jesus is right. If we were able to love God wholeheartedly and to love others as much as we love ourselves, we would be keeping God's law perfectly. We would be flawless and wouldn't need God's forgiveness or grace.

But, of course, on our own this kind of love isn't even possible. We can't love God wholeheartedly until he has changed our hearts, made them new, and aligned them to his will. God

made that clear to the Israelites in Deuteronomy 30:6: *"The LORD your God will circumcise your hearts and the hearts of your descendants, so that you may love him with all your heart and with all your soul, and live."* God's grace always precedes our ability to please him. So, without his help, we're hopeless.

But this expert in theology didn't want to admit to anything! The next thing out of his mouth should have been, "I haven't been able to do that, Jesus. What hope is there for me?" Instead, Luke tells us that, *"he wanted to justify himself, so he asked Jesus, 'And who is my neighbor?'" (Luke 10:29).*

The religious expert knew (as all people who look closely at their hearts know) that he hadn't loved God with an undivided heart, but a divided one. And he hadn't loved others as much as himself, but he'd put himself above them. But he didn't want to admit it!

This guy was looking for a loophole. He asked Jesus to clarify who *exactly* the word *neighbor* was referring to. This guy wanted eternal life on his terms, not on God's. So then, to shake him up, Jesus told the story we often call "The Good Samaritan."

HERE'S WHAT THE STORY'S ABOUT:

In Jesus' story, a man (who we can infer from the context was Jewish) is helped by a despised foreigner (a Samaritan), after being rejected by two of the respected religious leaders of his own people. Jesus brought the meaning of the story home by asking the religious expert a pointed question,

> *"Which of these three do you think was a neighbor to the man who fell into the hands of robbers?" The expert in the law replied, "The one who had mercy on him." Jesus told him, "Go and do likewise."* (Luke 10:36, 37)

The law expert couldn't even bring himself to say the word *Samaritan*. Instead, he just refers to him as "the one who had mercy."

I can just imagine what was going through this expert's head: *What! Be like him! But I don't even like Samaritans, and you want me to imitate him!*

And that was exactly the point. How could he love others as himself if he continued to despise them? If this didn't convict the guy that he hadn't loved others as he should have, I don't know what could!

Jesus' story was meant to pull the rug out so this guy wouldn't be able to justify himself, so that he'd realize his need to ask for and receive God's forgiveness! It's not just a story about "being nice."

The Samaritan gave up his **time** (by stopping to help), his **expertise** (by bandaging the man's wounds), his **money** (by paying for the man's convalescence), his **dignity** (by climbing down into the ditch), and his **comfort** (by allowing the man to ride his donkey in his place). That's what love looks like. That's loving others as you love yourself.

Compassion always finds a specific way to meet a specific need. If it doesn't, all it turns out to be is pity. And it looks just like the response of the priest and the Levite.

Remember, the law expert asked "Who is my neighbor?" not "How should I show love to others?" To dive deeper into this story, think about this:

- Explain how Jesus' story actually answers BOTH questions.
- Which story character(s) do you think Jesus wanted the religious expert to identify with? Why do you think that? How can you tell?

QuickTip #15 – Need I Repeat Myself?

Look for repetition in the stories you tell. Repetition is one of the best friends a children's storyteller ever had. Often, stories include patterns in which events occur a number of times (typically three times, with the last time being the "charm," or the time when things work out). That's the case with this story—three people come up to the guy in the ditch, and it's the third guy who ends up helping the hurt man. When you find repetition, it allows you to include the audience by giving them something to say or do whenever that part of the story rolls around! What refrain might you use in this story for the injured man when he calls repeatedly for help?

Telling This Story to Students Ages 3-7

Be aware that this story is violent. The man was beaten nearly to death and left naked and dying in a ditch. Decide how you'll handle the violence of this story. For younger children, you may wish to leave most of it out. If you're telling this story to older students, you'll probably want to include some of it. I prefer muting violence by using humor to make it less scary and personalized. (For an example of what I'm talking about, see the suggestions for retelling the story to 5th or 6th grade boys, on pages 45, 46.) You may wish to begin your lesson by telling or reading the following **fable.**

None of the other animals in the jungle liked Samantha the Snake. She was slippery and slithery and sneaky and mean. In fact, the other animals didn't just stay clear of Samantha; they kept their distance from all the other snakes as well. After all, everyone knew what snakes were like.

So one day, Fluffy the Bunny was hopping along the trail, taking some lettuce to Toby the Tortoise's birthday party. He was turning 100 years old, and Fluffy wanted to give him some fresh lettuce from the other side of the jungle.

Just then, a group of monkeys saw Fluffy. Now the monkeys weren't particularly cruel, but they did like to play tricks on the other animals. And when they saw Fluffy, they thought it would be fun to tease her. So, as quick as a wink, they dropped from the tree and snatched the pile of lettuce off her back.

"Eee! Eee! Eee!" they laughed as they jumped back up into the trees.

They didn't even realize they'd knocked Fluffy into a thornbush where she hurt her leg.

"Ouch!" she cried. "My leg! It hurts!" She tried to hop but couldn't. "And now, I'm going to be late for Toby's party!"

She lay there by the trail and waited. Well, pretty soon, Mitzy the Mouse came walking by.

"Please help me!" cried Fluffy. "The monkeys were here! And my leg hurts!"

When Mitzy heard the monkeys had been there, she thought maybe they were still around, hiding in the trees. And she didn't want them to steal her gift too. Mitzy was bringing Toby some blackberries! So Mitzy the Mouse started to worry. She said, "I can't help. I'm in a hurry!" And she ran away.

Soon after that, Spunky the Squirrel came running along the path.

"Please help me!" cried Fluffy. "My leg hurts!"

But Spunky didn't want to be late for the party either, or miss the fun. "See you there!" he yelled. "I gotta run!"

So he left too!

Just then, Fluffy heard someone else coming through the underbrush. Oh, good. Maybe someone will finally stop and help me, she thought.

But when she looked up, who do you think she saw? . . . Right, slithering toward her was Samantha the Snake. And Fluffy thought, Oh, no! I wish it was anyone other than her! She's probably going to bite me!

But Samantha didn't try to bite Fluffy at all. Instead, she slithered over and wrapped her long tail around Fluffy's leg so that it wouldn't hurt so bad. And then she told Fluffy, "Hug my neck with your paws-s-s-s . . . I'll take you to the party mys-s-s-self."

"I didn't know you were invited," said Fluffy.

"I was-s-s-sn't," said Samantha.

"Oh . . . well, where's your neck?" asked Fluffy.

"Between my head and my tail," said Samantha.

"I see," said Fluffy, holding on.

And then, Samantha the Snake took Fluffy all the way to the party. And no one bothered them, not even the monkeys because everyone kept their distance from Samantha! The monkeys returned the lettuce, and Toby had a wonderful party. Everyone was there!

"Please stay!" said Fluffy to Samantha.

And when everyone saw how kind Samantha had been, they changed their minds about her. They all had a great time. And all of the animals, including Samantha, are looking forward to Toby's next big birthday party. The end.

Say, **"God wants us to show love to others by helping them."**

Young children love to be involved in stories. When you teach them a story that they can retell with hand gestures or finger motions, it's typically called a **finger play** story. Listed below is a finger play for the story of "The Good Samaritan." Make up some fun, easy hand gestures to accompany it!

> **One** man walkin' down a dusty road
> Here come the robbers . . .
> And they took his clothes . . . (embarrassed) *AH!*
>
> **Second** man walkin' down a dusty road . . .
> Saw the hurt man,
> Left him all alone . . . (sadly) *Hm . . .*
>
> **Third** man walkin' down a dusty road . . .
> Does he stop and help?
> No, no, no! . . . (angrily) *Humph!*
>
> **Fourth** man walkin' down a dusty road . . .
> Helped him up,
> Gave him clothes.
> What a nice man on a dusty road!
> Made a new friend on a dusty road!

Jesus told the story of "The Good Samaritan" in a very specific context: a man wanted to justify his sin so that he could get to Heaven. This parable does two things: (1) reveals to him that he hasn't kept God's law perfectly, and (2) gives him a guide on how to live the way God intends.

When we retell this story to our students, we can try to accomplish the same two things Jesus did: (1) reveal to our students that they haven't kept God's law perfectly, and (2) give them a guide on how to live the way God desires.

With God's help, we can understand how we've failed to live his way, and—through the power of his Holy Spirit in our lives—we can begin to act in sync with God's will.

One way to set up the context of the story would be to bookend your telling of "The Good Samaritan" with the conversation between Jesus and the religious expert by sharing a **monologue**.

QuickTip #16 - Look for Connections!

Jesus' parents tried to stay at an inn when he was born, but there was no room. In the story of "The Good Samaritan," Jesus tells of an injured man recuperating at an inn. Whenever you find connections like this in Bible stories, it's fun to ask, "What if it were the same innkeeper? . . . What insights into love and the life of Jesus might he be able to offer?"

Then create a monologue of the innkeeper retelling the two stories ("The Birth of Jesus" and "The Good Samaritan") to some guests around his fireplace!

So there I was talking to Jesus, right? You know, the Teacher. The Rabbi. The Healer. And I ask him, I say, "How can I get into Heaven?" I figure he's the guy to ask! And I figure I've got it made since I know so much about the Bible and everything.

But then he says to me, he says, "What do you think? What's the Bible say?"

Well, of course, I know we're supposed to be perfect, you know—love God with all your heart and love your neighbor too. So that's what I say to him. And Jesus nods and says, "Good answer. Do that and you'll be all set."

But then, I'm thinking, *Um . . . well, I haven't always done that exactly, you know . . .* So I thought maybe there was a loophole or something. Maybe an escape clause somewhere in there for people like me. So I say to him, I say, "OK then, who's my neighbor?"

And that's when Jesus tells me this story . . .

(At this point, tell the story of "The Good Samaritan" in your own words, or have another person tell the story as if he were Jesus. Then conclude . . .)

So then he asks me, he says, "Who was the guy's neighbor?"
And I didn't even use the word *Samaritan*.
I couldn't. I couldn't say it.
So I say, I say to him, "The guy who showed mercy."
And then Jesus says, he says, "Go and do the same."
Huh. I need to be like a Samaritan? Who'd a-thought it . . .
But I don't even like those people!
Hm . . . But maybe that's his point.
I don't need to like 'em; I need to love 'em. Huh.
So, who is my neighbor?
The people I look down on.
I guess love isn't what you KNOW, after all . . . it's what you DO.
I got a lot to learn about love after all.

At the end of the story, the religious expert realized that he was supposed to have mercy on everyone, even those of another culture, background, or upbringing.

After the religious expert is finished, help the children (1) admit they haven't kept God's law of love, (2) ask God for forgiveness, and (3) ask God for help in showing real love to others.

Creative Connection Section		
Field Trip Ideas	This story begins on a dangerous, winding road and ends in a hotel. Consider retelling it in the lobby of a hotel, the waiting room of a hospital (since the wounded man was cared for medically at the hotel), or in a ditch next to a road.	
Mood and Atmosphere	(1) Dusty, sunny, desert-like conditions. (2) A comfortable hotel (or hospital) room.	
Sensory Connections	**Sight**	Show the children pictures of what narrow twisty roads along steep cliffs look like.
	Touch	Some objects that relate to this story include: robbers (signify with a bandanna), a wallet (the man was robbed), a set of clothes (including underwear!), bandages, a donkey, a desert road, two coins, a hotel (signify with a brochure of a hotel). Use any, or all, of them to help you retell the story! Pull your props out of a backpack the hurt guy might have been wearing!
	Hearing	You could reenact the guy getting robbed by holding up signs with comic-book-style fight words such as "Pow!" "Biff!" "Zowie!" "Wham!" "Crunch!" or even "I Want My Mommy!" Other sounds that relate to the story include: men walking, a donkey clomping, and the sun sizzling.
Costume Ideas	Either dress like a religious expert (think TV evangelist or a seminary professor) or like the wounded man who was stripped of his clothes. (You probably wouldn't want to tell the story dressed exactly like *that* . . . but you could wear a swimsuit and wrap a towel around yourself, or wear torn-up clothes!)	
Game Ideas	Often, when children play games, they're more concerned about winning than about serving the other team. Discuss how we should respond when a member of the other team gets hurt. How does good sportsmanship relate to the story of "The Good Samaritan"? How will this story change your attitude when you play games?	

TELLING THIS STORY TO STUDENTS AGES 8-12

Even though we don't know what the injured man said as he cried out for help, we can guess and create a refrain that he might have used. When the entire audience responds to a storyteller's cue, we call it a **call and response** story.

The Man Who Was Ditched
(a call and response version of "The Good Samaritan")

Notes for the storyteller: Divide the audience into two groups. The first group is the INJURED MAN GROUP. The second group is the UNHELPFUL HOLY PEOPLE GROUP. Explain each group's part to them and teach them the words to their refrain (see the story).

If you have a small group (or if you're telling the story to younger students), you may want to use only the INJURED MAN GROUP and say the other parts yourself. When it's time for the different groups to join in, nod and gesture to them so they know it's time to say their parts.

Don't worry about memorizing the storyteller's parts. Just use your own words to narrate the action of the story. You may, however, wish to memorize the short rhyme at the end of the story. Also consider adding gestures that the groups can do as they say their lines!

I've included some W.E.G.I. ideas in parentheses (in regular type) for retelling this story to 5th or 6th grade boys. Use 'em if you dare! (Stage directions and storytelling tips appear in parentheses and italics.)

STORYTELLER: **Once, a man was walking from Jerusalem to Jericho when he was attacked, beaten, and robbed! The thieves took his money. They took his coat. They even took his clothes! AH!** (*cross your arms in front of yourself like you're naked*) **They threw him in the ditch in his underwear . . . So as he lay there, he called and he called and he called for help . . .**

INJURED GROUP: **Anybody, anybody, please help me! I was beaten and robbed and I have an owie!**

STORYTELLER: **Soon a priest came by. Now, a priest back then was like a pastor is today. So if you were lying by the side of the road and your pastor came along, do you think he would stop and help you? Especially if you were in your underwear!? . . . So the man expected the priest to help him. But you know what happened instead . . .**

UNHELPFUL GROUP: **The priest walked by with his nose held HIGH, Pretending that he didn't hear the hurting man CRY.**

STORYTELLER: **Now, I gotta tell you, this guy was hurt really bad . . .** (*This part is for the 5th or 6th grade boys . . . I mean,* [*slowly and with feeling*] *his leg was broken and the bone was kinda stickin' through the skin there . . . and his ear was half-chewed off . . . and his stomach was ripped open . . . and his guts were hangin' out!*) **So he did the only thing he could do—he called and he called and he called for help . . .**

INJURED GROUP: **Anybody, anybody, please help me! I was beaten and robbed and I have an owie!** (*I've got a big owie right here with my guts hanging out . . .*)

STORYTELLER: **Soon a Levite came by. Now, a Levite back then was kinda like your Sunday school teacher today. So if you were lying there hurt by the side of the road, and your Sunday school teacher came along, do you think she would stop and help you? . . . Especially if you were in your underwear?! . . . So the guy thought for sure the Levite would help him. But you know what happened instead . . .**

UNHELPFUL GROUP: **The Levite walked by with his nose held HIGH, Pretending that he didn't hear the hurting man CRY.**

STORYTELLER: **By now, the guy was getting desperate! He was too weak to yell anymore. All he could do was whisper for help . . .** *(at this point, if you're using two groups, invite everyone to say the injured man's part together)*

INJURED GROUP: *(whispering)* **Anybody, anybody, please help me! I was beaten and robbed and I have an owie!** (My leg's broken . . . my ear's hangin' off . . . my guts are fallin' out . . . this has not been my day . . .)

STORYTELLER: **Well, that's when he saw the third man . . . a man he didn't like . . . it was a man from Samaria . . . Now, since he was a Jew, he hated people from there . . . 'cause they looked different and dressed different and worshiped God different than he did . . . he called 'em names . . . in fact, he'd spit every time he said the word** *Samaritan* **just to show how much he hated 'em.** (And when he saw the Samaritan, he was scared. 'Cause he knew, as a Jew, what he'd do if he found a hurt Samaritan by the side of the road . . . Maybe give him a couple quick kicks *[pretend to karate kick someone]* maybe even pull his guts the rest of the way out *[mime this disgusting action]*) . . . **He expected the Samaritan to walk past, or maybe even hurt him worse! But you know what happened instead . . .**

> **The Samaritan stopped. He offered his hand.**
> **He bandaged his wounds and he helped the man.**
> **He put him on a donkey, he took him to an inn,**
> **And he paid the innkeeper to take care of him!**
>
> **Now, the moral of the story, if you don't yet KNOW IT:**
> **Don't just say you love your neighbor, find a way to SHOW IT!**

See how the repetition of the story lends itself to using refrains? Also notice that I included a moral for the story. You may choose not to include it, but I like how it summarizes the story. Again, add in your own imagination, wording, and ideas.

Sometimes when a story is as familiar as this one, it's fun to retell it in an unexpected way and then discuss afterward the surprises or differences between the new version and the Bible's version. Listed below is a version of "The Good Samaritan" that includes a twist at the end.

W.E.G.I. (Weird & Extremely Goofy Ideas)

You may wish to stage a retelling of this story that includes a pillow fight (for the attack), fake blood (ketchup or spaghetti sauce), hosing off the man in the ditch (when the Samaritan cleans his wounds), and a ride on a real live donkey (played by one of the teachers!).

If you decide to include the pillow fight, be sure your students remove their glasses from their faces and sharp objects from their pockets before beginning. Otherwise, you may have a real injury to attend to!

The Good Samaritan Revisited[1]
(a "what if?" version of "The Good Samaritan")

Notes for the storyteller: I first wrote this story for a collection of sermon illustrations for youth pastors. You could read it as is, retell it in your own words, or even perform it as a **reader's theatre** piece.

To use as a reader's theatre script, make 5 photocopies of the story, then take a highlight marker and mark the speaking parts for (1) NARRATOR, (2) INJURED MAN, (3) PRIEST, (4) LEVITE, (5) LAST GUY TO ARRIVE. Cross off phrases like "the voice responded" or "whispered the man" since these speaker tags are necessary only in a written story and aren't needed for oral presentation. Hand out the scripts and get started!

One day a priest was walking down a country lane when he heard cries coming from a ditch on the other side of the road.

"Help me! Help me, please!"

The priest stopped and strained his neck to see into the ditch. Then he called across the road, "What happened to you?"

"I was traveling to town when I was attacked, beaten, and robbed. Please help me, I can't move," the voice responded.

The priest paused for a moment. Then he yelled back to the voice in the ditch. "Listen, there's this guy called the Good Samaritan who always helps people in need. He should be coming down the road anytime now. He'll help you. I don't know anything about first aid, and I wouldn't want to make things worse."

"Wait, you don't understand, I'm . . ."

But the priest had already gone on his way.

Soon another man came walking along the road. This man was a Levite.

"Help me! Help me, please!"

The Levite stopped in the road and looked from side to side. "Who was that? Who said that?"

"I did, over here!" called the voice from the ditch on the other side of the road.

"You talkin' to me?" asked the Levite.

"Yes, you! I was traveling to town when I was attacked, beaten, and robbed. I need your help!"

"Oh," said the Levite, gazing toward the ditch. "You do sound like someone who could use some help. Wait a minute! Attacked? Beaten? Robbed? What a coincidence. This reminds me of a story a fellow named Jesus told! Ever heard of him?"

"Yeah, I know the story. Now, can you help me?"

"Actually, I'm in quite a rush. But I'm sure that someone else will be along shortly to help you. Someone called . . . um . . . the Good Samaritan! That's it! He'll be along soon. This is a busy road, you know."

"Couldn't you help me? I'm feeling very weak. I can't . . ."

"I'm sorry, but I'm not the Good Samaritan. I'm the Levite. If I helped you, it would ruin the story. You wouldn't want me to do that, now would you?"

"No, I wouldn't want you to do that, but I think it's already . . . Wait! Come back!"

"Patience there, old chap! I'm sure the Good Samaritan will be along shortly," the Levite said, as he went on his way.

"Ohhhh . . . I can't last much longer," the wounded man said softly.

Soon another man came walking along the same road. He ran over to the ditch when he heard the man crying.

"Oh, my goodness! What happened?"

"I was traveling to town when I was attacked, beaten, and robbed. Two other men walked by and haven't helped me. Please help me. I can't move."

The traveler peered at the wounded figure lying on the ground in front of him. Finally, he said, "Wait a minute . . . you look familiar. Where are you from?"

[1] Reprinted from *Still More Hot Illustrations*, copyright 1999 by Youth Specialties, Inc., 300 South Pierce Street, El Cajon, CA 92092. www.YouthSpecialties.com. Used by permission.

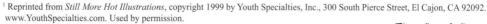

"Samaria."

"Do you by any chance have a nickname?" he asked, suddenly excited.

"Me? Oh, some people call me the Good Samaritan because I helped an injured man on this road awhile back."

"Yes! Yes! Well, sir, I was the man you helped! All this time I have been looking for you because I wanted to pay you back! Wow, this is great! I can't wait until I find my friends and tell them that I actually met up with you again! And now I can finally pay you back! Look, here are two silver coins—exactly what you gave that innkeeper. I feel so much better having finally repaid you. This is wonderful!"

The grateful man, who had himself once been attacked, beaten, and robbed, laid the two silver coins in the dust next to the wounded man and then cheerfully went on his way, whistling a happy tune.

"Wait, wait! I don't want your money, . . ." whispered the man from Samaria. But it was too late. The other man was already gone.

And so, the Good Samaritan died quietly in a ditch by the side of the road.

After you tell both "The Good Samaritan Revisited" and the story of "The Good Samaritan" found in the Bible, discuss these questions with your students:

1. Did you expect the "The Good Samaritan Revisited" to end the way that it did?
   Why or why not?
2. How did you feel at the end of the story? What made you feel that way?
3. How do you think the religious expert felt when Jesus' story was done? Why do you think that?
4. What was the most important thing to the first man who stopped? the second? the third?
   What was the most important thing to the injured man? What is most important to God?
5. How did this story differ from "The Good Samaritan" story found in the Bible?
   How was it the same? Were the messages of the two stories the same or different? How?
6. Discuss how showing mercy is different from feeling pity. You may not find someone dying by the side of the road, but how can you show mercy (vs. pity) to people in need whom you meet every day?

ADDITIONAL IDEAS AND LESSON CONNECTIONS:

To help your students put this story into practice, you may wish to do some **improvisational role-playing**.

To create your own improvisational situations based on a Bible story, first identify what the main point of the story is. For example, this story is about treating people of a different race, gender, political, or religious background with respect and compassion. What does real love look like? What does it really mean to love others as we love ourselves? To translate that into language kids of today can understand, you might say:

1. Don't pick on people who are different from you.
2. Don't look down on others.
3. Be nice to everyone, not just the people who are nice to you.
4. Be kind to the kids no one else likes.
5. Help people who are hurt, even if they're not your friends.

Then create situations that portray that principle!

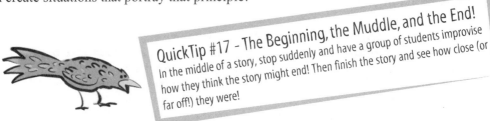

QuickTip #17 - The Beginning, the Muddle, and the End!
In the middle of a story, stop suddenly and have a group of students improvise how they think the story might end! Then finish the story and see how close (or how far off!) they were!

The Good SamarSKITan
(improvisational role-playing ideas for "The Good Samaritan")

Notes for the storyteller: Use the following improvisational drama activities to bring up issues related to the story of "The Good Samaritan." Each of the role-play situations explores aspects of the story. Discuss the improvisations before the close of class.

1. You and your friends are playing basketball when a new kid you don't know shows up. He looks a little weird. Act out what happens when he tries to join your game. (2–4 people)
2. Two kids are going to the park. Act out a scene of what happens when one kid's younger brother tries to tag along. Neither of the older two want him to come! (3 people)
3. Your mom was driving you to school when the car stalled by the side of the highway. After three hours, someone finally stops. Act out your conversation. (3 people)
4. Two people walk by a beggar. A father is trying to explain to his child why he didn't give the man any money. The boy doesn't understand. (2 or 3 people)
5. A couple of bullies have beaten you up and stolen your bike. Someone you always pick on and make fun of is coming your way—you don't know if she wants to help you or hurt you. Act out what happens. (2 people)
6. For the first time ever, you're chosen captain of a team! You get to pick teams! You want to pick one of your friends, but you notice a kid who always gets chosen last. You wonder if you should choose him. You friends will probably laugh at you if you do. Act out what happens. (2 or 3 people)
7. Johnny always plays by himself on the playground. One day you invite him to play kickball with you and your friends because you want to be nice. He swears at you and gets angry. Act out what happens next. (2 or 3 people)
8. You see your Sunday school teacher walk right by this one kid who is sitting in the corner, crying. You wonder if she saw him or ignored him. You decide to talk with her. Act out the conversation. (2 people)
9. Your mom has asked you to do the dishes tonight, even though it's your brother's night to help. Your brother claims he's sick. Act out what happens. (2 or 3 people)
10. Susie always pretends she's hurt or sick so she can spend time with the teacher. One day when she's crying, you and your friends laugh at her. She runs to the teacher. How do you feel? What do you do? (2–4 people)

PRAYER CONNECTION:
1. Pray for the courage to admit that you haven't kept God's laws and that you need his forgiveness.
2. Pray for the compassion and kindness to help those in need.
3. Pray for the ability to love even the unlovable.

INTERACTIVE PRAYER IDEA:
Hand out adhesive bandages to the children and have them place the bandages on their arms or wrists. Then, whenever they see them throughout the day, they can be reminded to pray for those who are hurting, lonely, or afraid! What a great way to be a good neighbor!

5 The Friend in the Night

BASED ON: Luke 11:5-13

BIG IDEA: We should pray with persistence and boldness, trusting in God's goodness to receive what we've requested.

GRACE CONNECTION: Our loving God is ready and willing to answer our prayers. He cares enough about us to give us good things, including the greatest gift of all—the Holy Spirit. Don't give up on God. He always responds to those who seek him.

> *If you then, though you are evil, know how to give good gifts to your children, how much more will your Father in heaven give the Holy Spirit to those who ask him!* (Luke 11:13)

TOPICS: Boldness, faith, God's character, Holy Spirit, persistence, prayer

MEMORY SPARKS: To find yourself in this story, think of a time when . . .
1. You gave up praying for something because God didn't seem to answer your prayer . . . What happened?
2. You made a request from someone even though you realized it was a bad time . . .
3. You felt like you might be annoying God with your requests . . .

To help your students connect with this story, say, "Think of a time when . . ."
1. You kept nagging your parents about something until they finally gave in and got it for you . . . Did they get it because they loved you or just so you'd stop bugging them?
2. Someone kept asking you to play with him, and you finally gave in just to get him off your back . . .
3. You wondered if God was really listening to your prayers . . . What happened?

HERE'S WHAT'S GOING ON:

> *One day Jesus was praying in a certain place. When he finished, one of his disciples said to him, "Lord, teach us to pray, just as John taught his disciples."* (Luke 11:1)

The disciples were obviously impressed by the passionate, personal way that Jesus talked with God. At last, one of his disciples asked him to give them some advice on how they should pray. Jesus obliged and shared with them a version of what has become known as the Lord's Prayer (even though this wasn't really how the Lord prayed, but rather a model for how the disciples should pray). Then Jesus launched into a story that further exemplified and clarified how his followers should pray.

HERE'S WHAT THE STORY'S ABOUT:

In Jesus' story, a man has received a late-night visitor. The guy has run out of food but wants to show hospitality to his guest. Now remember, this is before fast-food restaurants and 24-hour

supermarkets. So, he goes to his buddy's house and starts knocking on the door.

But his buddy doesn't want to get up. "Go away!" he says. "It's late! I'm in bed!" When the man won't stop knocking, the sleepy neighbor finally gets the food for him just so he can get some shut-eye.

It isn't his friendship that motivates him to give the man some bread—it's simply his desire to get some sleep! As Jesus summarized:

> *I tell you, though he will not get up and give him the bread because he is his friend, yet because of the man's boldness he will get up and give him as much as he needs. So I say to you: Ask and it will be given to you; seek and you will find; knock and the door will be opened to you. For everyone who asks receives; he who seeks finds; and to him who knocks, the door will be opened.* (Luke 11:8-10)

The man in the story asked, sought, knocked, and received. The door was opened to him. The door will also be opened to us. Remember, the context for all of this is the disciples' request that Jesus teach them how to pray. This story emphasizes that we should pray with boldness and persistence.

Now as you can probably tell, we're meant to identify with the man who came knocking in the middle of the night. God is represented in the parable by the friend who wants to get back to bed. Don't get too caught up here. Jesus isn't saying that God is fast asleep when we pray to him, or that he gets annoyed by our prayers and only answers them to shut us up. Jesus seems to have anticipated this misinterpretation of the story because in the next couple of verses he says,

> *Which of you fathers, if your son asks for a fish, will give him a snake instead? Or if he asks for an egg, will give him a scorpion? If you then, though you are evil, know how to give good gifts to your children, how much more will your Father in heaven give the Holy Spirit to those who ask him!* (Luke 11:11-13)

People aren't perfect. In fact, we're far from it: "evil" is the term Jesus uses here to refer to us. Yet we still know how to treat people kindly and grant their requests. If that's the case, then how much more will God (who *is* perfect!) give us the most wonderful gift of all—the Holy Spirit—when we ask?

We should be bold and persistent in our prayers, and we should also trust that God, out of his goodness, will answer our prayers. Faith must accompany our requests to God.

QuickTip #18 - To Boldly Go Where Few Have Gone Before!

Some students ask questions of their teachers when they don't understand something. Other students are too shy to do so. To help your students understand the aspect of boldness and persistence in prayer, you may wish to make up your own version of Jesus' story in which two students are considering asking their teacher to explain something, but one student is too timid to do so. Only the student who is bold enough to ask her teacher gets the answer and does well on the test. Act it out with 3 students!

TELLING THIS STORY TO STUDENTS AGES 3-7

When retelling this story to children, your challenge will be to help them understand that:

1. Jesus is using a comparison between how we act and how God acts to show us how assuredly God will answer our prayers.
2. We need to pray with persistence, boldness, and genuine faith.

You may wish to begin your lesson by telling or reading the following **fable.**

It was the middle of winter, and Mitzy the Mouse had a problem.

"Mitzy! Mitzy, wake up!"

"Who's there? Who is it?" she asked.

"It's me, Spunky the Squirrel," came the reply.

Mitzy hadn't seen Spunky for months. "What are you doing here?" she asked.

"An owl was trying to catch me all night," said Spunky. "I ran and ran and ran and finally came here. I'm hungry and I don't know where else to go. Now the owl is in my tree where my nuts are stored! I need some food!"

Mitzy looked around her home. She had a few seeds lying around, but not enough for a hungry squirrel.

"Please?" he asked.

Finally, Mitzy sighed. "OK, I'll get you some food."

But, since it was wintertime, many of the animals were fast asleep, hibernating until spring. Where would she get it?

Her friend Bucky the Badger could help, but he was sleeping in his tunnel beneath the meadow. She could hear him snoring, even through the ground! And when badgers go to sleep for the winter, you can't wake them up. They couldn't ask Bucky.

Her good friend George the Wolf was on the other side of the forest with the rest of the pack. And that was much too far for a mouse and a hungry squirrel to travel.

Hm . . . she thought. "What about Bryan the Bear? Maybe he can help us!" Bryan was a kind and helpful bear who usually stored extra nuts and berries in the back of his den.

"B-b-b-b-bear?" sputtered Spunky. "You wanna wake up a bear in the winter?! What if he's grouchy? Wha-wha-what if he . . . eats us up?"

"Bryan's my friend. He'll help us. I know he will. Come on."

So Mitzy and Spunky went to Bryan's cave.

But Spunky hid behind a tree while Mitzy went to wake Bryan up. "Bryan! Wake up!" she yelled. "Do you have any seeds or acorns or nuts you could share?"

A great big bear voice came rumbling out of the cave. "Go away! I'm asleep!"

"No, you're not, you're talking to me!"

"I must be talking in my sleep . . . Now, good night!"

Spunky was scared. "Let's get out of here, Mitzy! He's gonna eat us! I know it!"

"No, he won't. Trust me." She called into the cave again, "Bryan, please help us! Spunky is hungry! Can we have just a few nuts and berries?"

After a moment they heard Bryan's voice, "Is it really springtime already?"

"No. We just need a few nuts, and then you can go back to sleep. Please!" Mitzy just wouldn't give up. And finally, Bryan sighed and scooped up a paw-full of berries and nuts and brought them to Mitzy and Spunky.

"Have a nice midnight snack," he said. Because for Bryan, who slept all winter, it was the middle of the night.

"Thank you," said Mitzy.

"G-g-g-g-g-ood-bye," said Spunky.

But Bryan had already yawned and curled up again on the floor of his cave.

"Whew!" said Spunky. "He was nice after all."

"Yes," said Mitzy. "He was."

And so Mitzy and Spunky enjoyed the seeds and nuts, and that owl didn't get a meal at all that day.

And Bryan? Well, as far as I know, he didn't wake again until spring.

The end.

One way to engage younger students is through an **imaginary journey** to the site of the story you're about to tell. This technique works well when your story includes memorable sights, sounds, smells, or activities. And since this story happens at night, it's rich in sounds! You could introduce Jesus' parable about the friend who came at night by saying:

OK, kids! I want you to pretend that we're no longer in this room, but instead it's nighttime and we're walking through a village far away . . . (*walk in place*) **C'mon, let's go! . . .** (*if desired, turn off the classroom lights*)

Can you hear the night sounds? I think a hear a dog barking! (*put your hand up to your ear to encourage your students to make dog sounds*) **. . . And an owl hooting . . .** (*make owl sounds*) **and some frogs croaking . . . and the crickets . . . and—oh no! Look up there!** (*point up to the sky*) **A bat! Run! . . .** (*run in place*) **. . . Oh no, it's too dark to see where I'm going . . .** (*fall over as if you walked into a tree branch*) **Ouch! . . . It sure is dark . . .**

Whew! OK, climb over the fence . . . (*pretend to climb over a fence*) **. . . Hide behind that bush . . . and—oh my! I hear something else tonight! I hear people snoring . . .** (*snore really loudly*) **. . . But now, wait a minute . . . the snoring has stopped . . . look over there . . .** (*point to the side of the stage*) **. . . There's a man calling to his friend. He woke him up! I wonder what's going on?! Maybe there's a problem! I hope not! Let's all sit down and see what they're talking about here in the middle of the night!** (*gesture for the children the sit down quietly and listen*) **. . .**

> **QuickTip #19 - Remember to A.S.K.!**
> An easy way to remember the main points of this story is by remembering the acronym A.S.K.:
> **A**sk and you shall receive, **S**eek and you will find, **K**nock and the door will be opened to you!

After inviting the children to join you for the imaginary journey, tell Jesus' parable yourself, have a partner stand up on stage and tell it, or do a skit that reenacts the story!

This story has only a few characters. It also has a simple flow of action so it would be an easy story to learn, remember, and act out. If you do an imaginary journey (such as the one suggested above), you might want to transition directly into a **skit** in which you reenact the story. For example . . .

Late Night Delivery
(a skit based on "The Friend in the Night")

Notes for the storytellers: The following script uses contemporary names and references. Feel free to change them if you want to keep the story happening during Bible times. You'll need 3 frozen pizzas, a pair of pajamas, a funny sleeping cap, and 3 people for this skit. This would be a great story for some teenage volunteers to act out!

Cast: BONNIE, THE FRIEND (girl or boy—you're perky and excited!), GEORGE, THE SLEEPY GUY (preferably a boy—you're sleepy and a little grouchy!), BABY (girl or boy—you're offstage and wail like a baby!)

(*This skit begins as BONNIE enters. GEORGE is either curled up and asleep onstage, or offstage snoring.*)

TEACHER:	**Lights! . . . Camera! . . . Action!**	BONNIE:	**I need a favor! You got a couple of frozen pizzas I can borrow?**
BONNIE:	**Hey! Hey, George, wake up! Wake up!**	GEORGE:	**What? It's the middle of the night!**
GEORGE:	(*enter, yawning, wearing pajamas and a big funny sleeping cap*) **Hey, what's going on?**	BONNIE:	**I know, but a friend of mine just showed up from Alaska, and he's starved!**

GEORGE: *(yawning)* **Well, go to the store or something. I'm going to bed.** *(turn, as if you're leaving)*

BONNIE: **Listen, I tried all the stores and all the restaurants and everything. They're all closed.**

GEORGE: **Closed?**

BONNIE: **Yeah! I think it's a holiday or something. Please, can you help us out here?**

GEORGE: **No way! Now, go home! I already tucked my kids in bed, and if you're not quiet, you're gonna wake up the baby.**

(from offstage—"WAAAA!")

GEORGE: **Oh, great. Now you've done it.**

(from offstage—louder this time, "WAAAA!")

BONNIE: **Listen, I'm not going home until you help me out.**

(from offstage—REALLY loud this time, "WAAAA!")

GEORGE: **OK, alright already! Here!** *(toss a frozen pizza at BONNIE)*

BONNIE: *(picking up the pizza)* **Thanks! You're a real pal!**

GEORGE: *(throw her the two remaining pizzas)*

BONNIE: **Wow. Three for the price of none. I knew you'd help me! Thanks!** *(exit)*

(from offstage—"WAAAA!")

GEORGE: **Yeah, well, I just hope the baby doesn't need changing.**

(from offstage—"WAAAA! I DO! I GOT A MESSY DIAPER!")

GEORGE: **Oh, great . . .**

(from offstage—"WAAAA! I WANNA PIZZA TOO!")

GEORGE: **Oh, brother . . .** *(exit)*

(Fade the lights out.)

After the skit say something like, **"Give 'em a hand, kids! . . . In that story, the sleepy guy gave his friend the pizzas because his friend was bold enough to ask for 'em, and he wouldn't give up.**

Jesus once told a story like that. He wanted people to think about this: If even humans treat people kindly and give 'em what they ask for, how do you think our perfect God who awesomely loves us is gonna respond when we ask him for stuff? *(allow them to respond)* **Right! God will give us the good things we ask for. Jesus said it this way:**

> *Which of you fathers, if your son asks for a fish, will give him a snake instead? Or if he asks for an egg, will give him a scorpion? If you then, though you are evil, know how to give good gifts to your children, how much more will your Father in Heaven give the Holy Spirit to those who ask him!* (Luke 11:11-13)

When we pray we should pray believing that God will answer us! Let's join together in a prayer right now! If the setting is appropriate, you may want to take this opportunity to explain the gospel to your children and encourage them to pray for the Holy Spirit, just as Jesus talked about in these verses.

		Creative Connection Section
Field Trip Ideas		This story occurs in a neighborhood at night. You could turn off the classroom lights to create a nighttime atmosphere, or even stand outside the classroom window and tell the story to the children inside, just like the guy who called to his friend in the story! Many stores are closed on Sunday mornings. Since the man in the story couldn't get food at a store and had to go to his friend's house, you could also tell this story in front of a closed grocery store, bakery, or restaurant.
Mood and Atmosphere		Cool, dark, sleepy, calm, and quiet . . . until the friend arrives!
Sensory Connections	**Sight**	Set out sleeping bags and pillows and let your students lounge on them as you tell the story.
	Touch	Some objects that appear in this story (and its explanation) include: a door, bread, pillows, fish, snakes, eggs, scorpions, and a wrapped up present to represent the Holy Spirit! Pull your props out of a lunch box, a grocery bag, or a shopping cart!
	Hearing	Any songs about friends (especially annoying friends!) would work well for this story. You could play a CD of sound effects of crickets or other soft nighttime sounds to set the mood for this story.
	Taste	Handing out fresh bread, donuts, cookies, or other baked goods will help the children get a handle on (and their lips on!) this story.
	Smell	The smell of freshly baked bread or warm chocolate chip cookies will help the students visualize the story. (Be sure to serve 'em after the parable!)
Costume Ideas		You could tell this story dressed in pajamas and a nightcap and carrying your teddy bear!
Game Ideas		Persistence with God pays off. Think of a game in which boldness, persistence, and risk-taking pay off and playing it safe doesn't. Then play the game as an application of the principles woven into this story!

TELLING THIS STORY TO STUDENTS AGES 8-12

You might wish to have one of the story characters tell the story from his or her point of view. When a character from a story tells the story from his or her perspective, it's called a **monologue**. You could tell the story from the perspective of one of the man's sleepy children, his wife, the hungry guy who arrived so late, or a cranky neighbor. However, since we're meant to identify with the man who came knocking on his buddy's door, he would be the most natural one to choose.

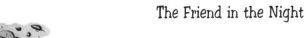

You Can Count on Al!
(a monologue of "The Friend in the Night")

Notes for the storyteller: When you present a **monologue**, it's best to have something to do while you talk. Suggested actions for this monologue are provided throughout the script.

The story is purposely told mostly in the present tense to give the impression that someone is remembering it.

Also, when you're telling a story, you don't typically say "he said" or "she replied" all the time. You just leave those speaker tags out and signify who's talking by the way you stand, the voice inflection you use, or the direction in which you look when you speak. Practice this story a few times before performing it so that you can be sure you don't mix up the voices of the Narrator, Al, and Billy Bob.

(Walk up front carrying two grocery bags. Pull out stuff to make some sandwiches—such as a long piece of unsliced French bread, cheese, lettuce, tomatoes, mayo, a serrated knife, etc. . . . If you want to be a little silly, pull out some unexpected items too, such as pickles, beets, bananas, and candy bars.)

So there I am, getting ready for bed, when I hear a knock at my door. And I'm thinkin', *Who can that be knocking at my door? Go away. Don't come 'round here no more . . .*
(begin making your sandwich by cutting the bread in half lengthwise as you talk)
But the knocking continues, so I open up the door, and it's my old friend Billy Bob from out of town.
"Hey, Billy Bob!"
(as Billy Bob) **"Yo."**
And I'm like, "C'mon in, Billy Bob. I'll get you some supper."
And Billy Bob was like, "Yo!"
(continue making your sandwich)
But then I look around, and I realize I'm out of food. Not a bite to eat in the whole place. And let me tell you, Billy Bob can eat! He eats so much we usually call him Billy Bib! So I think to myself, *Where am I gonna get food at this time of night? All the stores are closed* **. . . but then, I remember my pal Al.**
He's always come through for me in the past. So I figure he'll help us. If anyone will, Al will.
"Let's go to Al's," I said. "You can count on Al."
And Billy Bob was like, *(as Billy Bob)* **"Yo."**
(add more stuff to your sandwich)
So, I go over and knock on Al's door until I wake him up. "Hey, lemme borrow three loaves of bread!" I yell.
He's like, "It's late."
"I know!" I say. "But Billy Bob just showed up! And he's hungry!"
"You mean Billy Bib?"
(as narrator) **"Yup."**
(as Billy Bob) **"Yo."**
(as Al) **"Oh."**
Al didn't say anything for a while, but I knew he'd come through. Then, suddenly, he disappears into the house, and a few seconds later, this loaf of bread *(hold up the bread)* **comes sailing out the window and hits me on the head.**
(rub your head) **"Ow."**
(as Billy Bob) **"Yo!"**
(as Al) **"Wait, did you say THREE loaves?"**
"Yup."
(as Al) **"Why three?"**
"Billy Bob, remember?"
(as Al) **"Oh, yeah."**

And then, two more loaves come flyin' out.

(as Billy Bob) **"Yo! . . . Yo!"**

(start closing up the jar of mayo and putting stuff away)

So Al came through for us, just like I knew he would. He's that kind of guy. You can count on Al . . .

Well, I gotta go. Billy Bob's waiting for his sandwich. He already ate those other two loaves.

(Cut your sandwich in two slices, one tiny one and one huge one. Hold up the small one.) **This one's for me.**

(hold up the huge one) **And this one's for Billy Bob.**

(as Billy Bob) **"Yo . . . I mean . . . Yummy!"**

So, anyway, If you don't have a friend like Al, you should. He's the best friend a guy could have. Everyone needs a friend like Al. You can count on Al.

(as Billy Bob) **"Yo!"**

(walk offstage munching on your sandwich)

After this monologue you'll want to explain or read Jesus' story in your own words (use the script on the following page if you wish). Talk about the connections between the stories and the application of the parable to our lives today.

QuickTip #20 - Location, Location, Location!

Places often cue strong memories. Use this to your advantage when teaching Bible stories by retelling the story in another location. For example, since the story of "The Sower and the Four Soils" happens on a farm, it would make sense to tell it in a farmer's field . . . "The Friend in the Night " happens on the front step of a house at night. It would be a great story to tell at camp, on the porch of a cabin . . . "The Wise and Foolish Builders" occurs on a seashore—maybe plan a field trip to a nearby beach or retell this story at camp near the swimming lake!

When exploring each story, ask:

1. Where does this story take place?
2. Are there places nearby that relate to this story?
3. What advantages or disadvantages would there be to traveling somewhere else to tell this story?
4. What plans am I going to make?

W.E.G.I. (Weird & Extremely Goofy Ideas)

For a great attention-getting activity, have a person interrupt your lesson (either by banging on the door or knocking on your window), asking to borrow a stapler (or three candy bars!). At first, tell him to go away. Pretend you're angry at him! Have it prearranged for the person to keep interrupting your class over and over. Get more and more angry!

Finally, give him what he wants. Say something like, **"I'm only giving this to you so you'll quit bugging us!"**

Afterwards, talk about the situation with the children. Discuss why you gave him the object and then say, **"Let's look at a story Jesus told that's an awful lot like what just happened here in our class . . ."**

QuickTip #21 - Whose Story Is This, Anyway?

When creating monologues, find the person in the story whom we, the listeners, are meant to identify with, and then tell the story from his or her perspective. It'll make the application of the story to the lives of the listeners even easier!

Often, children in elementary school and middle school like to listen to and tell scary stories at sleepovers or campouts. It can be fun to pretend that you're going to tell a scary story, but then make it funny instead. Here's a "scary" **contemporary retelling** of this parable for preteens

The Nighttime Visitor (ooh . . . scary . . .)
(a contemporary retelling of "The Friend in the Night")

Notes to the storyteller: Kids love scary stories, but they don't REALLY want to be scared. So play this story up like it's gonna be really scary, and then have fun with it. Practice retelling this story a few times in your own words before telling it to your students. When you're ready to tell the story, turn off the lights and have everyone sit on the floor, close together.

OK, now, this story is really scary . . . I hope you don't get too scared . . . *(They'll say stuff like "We won't!" or "Yeah, right!" Keep telling 'em how scary it's gonna be . . .)*

So, once there was this guy, who lived not too far from here. His name was . . . *(say his name in your best scary voice)* **Luigi . . .** *(pause)* **And one night he was at home . . . by himself . . .** *(say "his room" in your best scary voice)* **. . . in his room! . . .**

Are you scared yet? *(they'll say "No!")* **Oh, you will be! . . .**

Outside his window, the night sounds came alive . . . Wind was howling through the forest . . . Owls were hooting from the treetops . . . Bats were winging their way through the raven-black darkness . . .

And all the while, Luigi lay there asleep, thinking he was safe . . . *(make snoring sounds)* **. . . When all of a sudden . . .** *(say this next part really slowly, and lean toward the kids as you say it)* **. . . he heard this noise right outside his window . . .** *(scream really loudly and jump toward the kids!)* **AHHH!**

So he sat up and looked out the window . . . and there, in the moonlight, he could see the figure of a man. And Luigi was really freaked 'cause the guy didn't walk away, and he looked like he had a knife in his hand . . .

The night sounds got quiet. Luigi gulped.

(scared) **"Who are you?" he asked.**

And the guy in the moonlight said . . . *(pause)* **"It's me, Lenny! I was wondering if I could borrow a pizza?"**

"What?! I thought you were a burglar or something!"

"Naw. I just got the midnight munchies!"

(in your best scary voice) **And then, Luigi gave him a pizza, Lenny used the knife to cut it, and he walked off into the night, with mozzarella cheese hanging from his chin . . .**

And some people say that even to this very day, in that neighborhood, when the moon is full and the wind is howling through the treetops, you can still hear Lenny's voice . . . *(lean really close to the students and say in a scary voice)* **. . . "I want a pizza . . . I want a pizza! I want a pizza . . .** *(scream really loud and jump toward the kids!)* **. . . FROM YOU!"**

I know that was pretty scary. I hope you didn't get too scared. *(They'll say stuff like "That wasn't scary!" or "Yeah, right!")*

OK, so I admit it—that wasn't really all THAT scary.

But you know what IS scary? How much this story is like one Jesus told long ago . . . Open up your Bibles with me to Luke 11:5-13, and let's take a look at Jesus' story and what it has to do with us today . . .

The Old Testament contains lots of stories of men and women who went boldly before God to make requests. For example:

- In Joshua 10:11-13 Joshua prayed that the sun would stand still in the sky . . . and it did!
- In 1 Samuel 1:10-20 Hannah prayed that she would have a baby . . . and she did!
- In 2 Kings 20:8-11 Isaiah prayed that the sun would go backward . . . and it did!

The main idea of this story is that persistence in prayer pays off. So think of an example from your life when you approached God boldly and it paid off. Share that story in your own words to let the children know that God hasn't changed and that he still answers our prayers today. Tell your students, **"Never think that God is too busy for you or that he doesn't want to hear about your problems. He cares about everything that happens in your life, both big and small."**

Let us then approach the throne of grace with confidence, so that we may receive mercy and find grace to help us in our time of need. *(Hebrews 4:16)*

Prayer Connection:

1. Pray for the courage to approach God with big, bold prayers.
2. Pray for the faith to believe in God's promises, even when he seems silent.
3. Pray for the Holy Spirit to fill and guide your life.

Interactive Prayer Idea:

Break off pieces of bread and eat them as you take turns praying. Talk about little prayer requests (crumbs) and big requests (loaves). Remind your students that God will listen and answer your prayers no matter how big or small they are!

6 The Foolish Rich Man

BASED ON: Luke 12:13-21

BIG IDEA: You cannot serve both God and materialism (Luke 16:13).

GOSPEL CONNECTION: Our relationship with God should be the most important thing in our lives. If we place ourselves first, we'll lose everything. But if we place our relationship with God first, we'll gain more than we could ever imagine. In this story, the rich man left God out of his vision for success and ended up losing everything. Don't let materialism pull you away from God. You cannot serve them both:

> *What good is it for a man to gain the whole world, yet forfeit his soul?*
>
> *(Mark 8:36)*

TOPICS: Consequences, distractions, greed, judgment, materialism, Pharisees, priorities, wealth

MEMORY SPARKS: To find yourself in this story, think of a time when . . .

1. You had big plans for your life, but they didn't include God . . .
2. You were busy thinking of yourself when God suddenly gave you a wake-up call . . .
3. You got so involved planning for your *future* that you forgot to serve God *today* . . .

To help your students connect with this story, say, "Think of a time when . . ."

1. You couldn't wait for Christmas because of all the toys you were gonna get . . .
2. You went through a stage when you separated all of your stuff from your siblings' stuff . . .
3. You wanted to get a certain toy or game just because everyone else was getting it . . .

HERE'S WHAT'S GOING ON:

A huge crowd had gathered to hear Jesus. Thousands of people were there *"trampling on one another" (Luke 12:1)*. Yet Jesus turned to his disciples and shared a series of warnings and encouragements with *them*, instead of with the crowd. Then, in the middle of eavesdropping on Jesus' discourse with his followers, a guy from the crowd interrupted Jesus, asking him to arbitrate an inheritance disagreement.

> *Jesus replied, "Man, who appointed me a judge or an arbiter between you?"*
> *Then he said to them, "Watch out! Be on your guard against all kinds of greed; a man's life does not consist in the abundance of his possessions."*
>
> *(Luke 12:14, 15)*

The guy who interrupted him wasn't thinking about Jesus' sermon, only his own inheritance! Greed had distracted him. Then Jesus told a story to that man and the rest of the crowd.

A rich landowner had a bumper crop one year. He decided to manage his good fortune wisely, invest carefully, plan for the future, retire early, take it easy, and enjoy life.

Sounds pretty good, huh? Not to God.

> *But God said to him, "You fool! This very night your life will be demanded from you. Then who will get what you have prepared for yourself?" This is how it will be with anyone who stores up things for himself but is not rich toward God.*
>
> *(Luke 12:20, 21)*

Whoa. That's pretty blunt. You store up things for yourself, and you're gonna lose it all. We should strive instead to be rich toward God. Our relationship with God is what matters most.

So is it wrong to plan for the future? Not necessarily. For a good insight into what's going on below the surface of this story, count up how many times the words *I, me,* or *self* appear  in Luke 12:16-20! The entirety of this man's life, plans, and priorities revolved around himself. In contrast, Jesus wants our lives, plans, and priorities to revolve around God.

> **QuickTip #22 - Stop Thinking About the Wording, Focus on the *Sounding*!**
> Rather than focusing on the progression of words in a story, practice the story orally and listen for the progression of sounds. Listen for words that work orally, even if they don't look quite right when you write them down. Strive to include phrases that flow well, sound right, and echo with rhythm and musicality.

Immediately following the story, Jesus told his disciples not to worry about their lives. Note the parallels he draws: *"Consider the ravens: They do not sow or reap* [the rich guy reaped a big crop], *they have no storeroom or barn* [the rich guy planned to build big barns to store his crops]; *yet God feeds them* [the rich guy wanted to feed himself]*" (Luke 12:24).*

Then Jesus summarizes: we should stop seeking the things of this world and pursue treasures in Heaven. The rich guy set his heart on what he would eat and drink in his retirement, but Jesus said, *"Do not set your heart on what you will eat or drink; do not worry about it" (Luke 12:29)*. The rich guy thought of himself first, but Jesus said, *"But seek his [God's] kingdom, and these things will be given to you as well" (Luke 12:31)*. All of these contrasts grow out of the story Jesus just told!

By the way, note that in Jesus' story, God asks the foolish rich guy, "When you're dead, who's gonna get your inheritance?" (See Luke 12:20.) Remember that man's inheritance question that prompted Jesus' story in the first place? Pretty slick how Jesus turned the tables, huh? Jesus certainly is the master storyteller!

The big question concerning Jesus' parable is not "Was it true?" but rather "Will it be told about me?"

TELLING THIS STORY TO STUDENTS AGES 3-7

Be aware that, as is, this story doesn't have a happy ending. It's not intended to make us feel good, but rather to shake us up. Now, you don't want to scare or traumatize young children with this story, so be careful to tell it in context and include Jesus' reassurances that come later in the chapter:

> *Do not be afraid, little flock, for your Father has been pleased to give you the kingdom.*
>
> *(Luke 12:32)*

God loves us and is gracious to us. When we trust in him, we don't need to live in fear, but with confidence.

You may wish to introduce this story by talking about how much God takes care of us all each day (Luke 12:22-34; see also Matthew 6:25-33). Here's a sample of what you might say, as well as suggested ideas for **props** (underlined) you could hold up while you speak . . .

Some people in our world today spend lots of time thinking about what they're gonna eat . . . *(hold up a* <u>fork</u>*)* . . . Other people spend lots of time thinking about what they're gonna wear . . . *(hold up a* <u>sweater</u>*)* . . . or where they're gonna live . . . *(a set of* <u>keys</u>*)* . . . or work . . . *(a* <u>cell phone</u>*)* . . .

Some people spend so much time thinking about those things that they don't think about God! . . . *(a* <u>Bible</u>*)* . . . They put themselves first instead of putting God first.

And kids, this happens to all of us sometimes. *(a* <u>mirror</u>*)* . . .

When Jesus talked about what's really important, he said . . .

Do birds . . . *(a toy* <u>bird</u>*)* . . . worry about tomorrow? Do they have to plant seeds? . . . *(a packet of* <u>seeds</u>*)* . . . Do they have to harvest crops? . . . *(a* <u>potato</u>*)* . . .

Do birds build barns to store their food? . . . *(a bird's nest or toy* <u>barn</u>*)* . . . No, of course not! And God takes care of them. God loves us more than birds! So, will he take care of us too? . . . *(the* <u>mirror</u>*)* . . . Yes! He will!

And what about pretty little flowers? . . . *(a* <u>flower</u>*)* . . . Do they have to go to work each day and earn money? *(a* <u>dollar bill</u>*)* . . . No, of course not! Do they weave clothes for themselves? . . . *(a* <u>sweater</u>*)* . . . No, but God gives them lovely colors to wear! If God does all that for flowers, then he's gonna take care of us even more! *(the* <u>mirror</u>*)* . . .

So, kids, do you think we should worry about how much food we're gonna have . . . *(the* <u>fork</u>*)* . . . or how much milk we're gonna get . . . *(a milk* <u>carton</u>*)* . . . or how many different sets of clothes we have? . . . *(the* <u>sweater</u>*)* . . .

Nope. We should trust in God to take care of us as we put him first in our lives! . . . *(the* <u>Bible</u>*)*

After introducing the story, retell the parable of "The Foolish Rich Man." Emphasize how important it is to put God (instead of ourselves) first in our lives and to trust in him (instead of ourselves) to take care of us. Listed below is a **story dramatization** of this parable. By the way, you'll need another helper to be the voice of God later in this story!

Jesus once told a story about a man who had a big farm. Kids, let's pretend that we're working hard on a farm . . . Toss some seeds out into the field . . . OK, hoe up the ground . . . Wait for it to grow . . . *(yawn)* . . . It's taking a long time . . . Let's go to sleep and see if it grows then . . .

Oh . . . look at that! The corn grew! *(measure the corn stalk with your arms)* . . . Now, what will we do? Let's pick it! OK, everyone . . . pick your corn . . . There's a lot of corn . . . Pick more . . . and more . . . and more! . . . It's hard to carry it all! . . . It's piled up to the ceiling! . . .

(fall over)

Alright, well, let's try to pack it all into our barns . . . Does it fit? No . . . Well then, let's pack it harder . . . Does it fit now? . . . OK, push it in there! . . . One more time, push hard, harder, harder! . . .

Hm . . . We seem to have a problem . . . What are we gonna do? . . . We could give some away . . . We could feed people who are hungry . . . We could sell the corn . . .

But today let's pretend we're being really GREEDY and we don't want to help other people! Grab all the corn for yourself! Let's build bigger barns and keep it all for OURSELVES!

(This next section is a conversation between the storyteller and God. It would probably be best if the person playing God is hidden from view.)

(voice of God) **"You'll be sorry!"**
Who's that?
(voice of God) **"It's me, God!"**
It sounds like _____! *(insert the name of your helper)*
(voice of God) **"Use your imagination!"**
Oh. OK.
(voice of God) **"Don't put yourself first! Don't be so greedy! You'll be sorry!"**
Aw, forget you, God! We'll do what we want!

C'mon, kids! Gather all that corn around yourself and curl up. Let's go to sleep, and in the morning we'll start work on our new barns . . .

(voice of God) "I warned you!"

OK, kids, let's stop pretending for a minute. Do you know that in Jesus' story, the man never woke up? I'm very sad to say he died in his sleep that night. And Jesus said that's how it'll be for all people who think only of themselves and refuse to put God first.

(voice of God) "Yeah, put me first!"
Um, we wanna put **THE REAL GOD** first. You can come out now, _____!
(insert the name of your helper. . . then she comes out)

How many of you know we should put God first in our lives? Right! Let's close with a prayer and ask him to help us do that right now!

		Creative Connection Section
Field Trip Ideas		Tell this story in a graveyard. Talk about the brevity of life and the importance of putting God first today.
Mood and Atmosphere		Pretty intense.
Sensory Connections	Sight	Hold up a coin. Read the words *In God we trust.* Discuss how true (or untrue) that is in our country today. Is it ironic that these words appear on our coins? Why or why not? Pull your props out of a pillowcase (the guy died in his sleep) or . . . a coffin! (For younger kids use a toy barn or something similar so they're not too frightened!)
	Touch and Taste	Pass around and nibble on some cereal made with corn, wheat, oats, barley, or something else the man might have grown.
	Hearing	Harvesting . . . snoring . . . party music . . . funeral music . . .
	Smell	OK, this is kinda gross, but it would be effective—find some roadkill. Bring it (or a picture of it) to class, or take a field trip to see it. Then read Psalm 49:12: *"But man, despite his riches, does not endure; he is like the beasts that perish."* Tie it into the story.
Costume Ideas		A modern parallel to the rich man might be a famous sports hero or rock star who lives only for himself. Dress up like one of these characters and deliver a monologue based on Jesus' story.

TELLING THIS STORY TO STUDENTS AGES 8-12

Consider starting class by retelling the ancient Greek myth of King Midas. (You may wish to replace the traditional version of him getting his wish from Bacchus, the god of wine, to a more generic genie lamp!)

In the story, King Midas wishes for the ability to turn all that he touches into gold. At first he loves it! He turns the rocks on the path and his house and his furniture to gold. But then he tries picking a flower (it turns golden and brittle) . . . and lying down to take a nap (his bed becomes golden and hard) . . . and eating supper (his food turns into gold). . . . You may wish to have him (and the audience) say this refrain each time he turns something into gold:

Twinkle, twinkle little gold,   *I'll keep all this for myself!*
I wish I had more to hold!   *Twinkle, twinkle, little gold,*
I will store it on a shelf!   *[I'm] glad my name's not Leopold!*

However, he soon discovers he'll never be able to pick a rose again, or be comfortable lying down, or even be able to eat or drink anything, ever again. . . . Finally, when his daughter walks in, he unthinkingly gives her a hug. . . . Only then does he realize that what he first thought was a blessing is really a horrible curse!

In some versions of the myth, he gets her back when he gives up his gift of turning things to gold. In other versions, he never gets her back. With your students, explore the parallels and similarities between Jesus' story and this ancient myth.

Sometimes it's fun to retell a story as a **rebus**. In a rebus, some words are replaced by pictures. Then, when children read the story, they insert the name of the object that the picture represents. For example (photocopy this and hand it out to your students):

Say, **"Jesus wanted everyone to store treasure in Heaven where it will never wear out, get used up, or rust away. Where is your treasure? Where is your heart? Where is your piggy bank?"** . . .

Where Is Your Piggy Bank?
(a creative retelling of "The Foolish Rich Man" with props)

Notes for the storyteller: Before performing this story, gather the suggested **props** and practice telling the story a few times.

To begin, walk onstage carrying two piggy banks. One should have a few coins in it, the other is empty. Have plenty of change in your pocket to deposit into the EARTHLY piggy bank (the HEAVENLY one stays empty the whole time).

You may wish to label the piggy banks: Earthly Treasures and Heavenly Treasures. You'll also need a hammer! You'll want to make sure the hammer is hidden nearby where the children won't see it.

What to say:	What to do:
Once upon a time there was a rich man who had lots of stuff.	SHAKE the EARTHLY bank.
Whenever he got a chance, he would store things up for a rainy day . . .	DEPOSIT change into the EARTHLY bank.
Most people thought he was really rich!	SHAKE the EARTHLY bank.
But in his heart, he was pretty poor. In fact, he was bankrupt . . .	SHAKE the HEAVENLY bank.
Well, one year his crops did really well!	DEPOSIT change into the EARTHLY bank.
I mean, really well!	DEPOSIT more change into the EARTHLY bank.
I mean, he had more crops than he knew what to do with!	DEPOSIT lots more change into the EARTHLY bank.
But, instead of thinking of God . . .	SHAKE the HEAVENLY bank.
Or thinking of others . . .	SHAKE the HEAVENLY bank.
He thought only of himself . . .	SHAKE the EARTHLY bank.
I'll store up all this stuff for me! he thought.	DEPOSIT lots of change into the EARTHLY bank.
Then I'll have plenty of money and good things saved up for when I'm old!	SHAKE the EARTHLY bank.
But God looked down from Heaven and said, "Sir, I believe it's time to cash in your piggy banks."	SHAKE the HEAVENLY bank.
That night God took the rich man's life.	Pull out a hammer and SMASH the EARTHLY bank.
"Now," said God. "Let's see what you've stored up for yourself for the life to come." . . .	SHAKE the HEAVENLY bank.
"And this," said Jesus, "is how it will be with anyone who stores up things for himself . . .	Hold up the shattered pieces of the smashed bank.
. . . but is not rich toward God."	SHAKE the HEAVENLY bank.

Say, **"Jesus said, *'For where your treasure is, there your heart will be also'"* (Luke 12:34).** **How can you expect to store treasure in Heaven when your heart is running after the things of earth? Love is the currency of Heaven. Selfishness is the currency of earth. Whatever you love, you treasure. Whatever you cherish, you seek. So, is it God? Or is it the things of this world?"**

Have your students fill in the following sentence, **"If only I had _____, then I'd be happy."** Discuss the ways people try to find happiness (for example, money, success, or popularity).

Ask, **"What does Jesus say in Luke 12:29-31 is the most important thing of all? Where does Jesus say we should store our treasures?"** (See Luke 12:33, 34.)

To further explore the issues of envy, success, wealth, and selfishness, check out Ecclesiastes 4:4 and James 4:1-4.

Then commit yourselves in prayer to living out Jesus' commands.

QuickTip #23 - Unhappily Ever After?
Stay true to the story you're telling. Not every story is meant to have a happy ending. Many of Jesus' stories have tragic, surprising, unsettling, or even horrifying endings. Be faithful to the way Jesus intended his stories to end and the impact he intended them to have. Don't try to make every story end happily ever after. Not all stories (or lives) do.

W.E.G.I. (Weird & Extremely Goofy Ideas)
Have your students make up their own disgusting verses to the song "The Worms Crawl In." Have the final verse reiterate the main point of Jesus' story!

PRAYER CONNECTION:
1. Pray that you might be rich toward God and stop living for yourself.
2. Pray for the ability to watch out for (and avoid) all kinds of greed.
3. Pray for the wisdom to know how to keep God first in all areas of your life.

SUGGESTED PRAYER FOR OLDER STUDENTS:
Read Psalm 39:4-7, 11-13 or have students take turns reading it line by line. After each line, exhale together as a reminder that our lives are as short as a breath. Pray for the right perspective and priorities!

The Great Banquet

BASED ON: Luke 14:16-24[1]

BIG IDEA: God's invitation to enter his kingdom has been extended to you. Don't refuse him.

GOSPEL MOTION: God's kingdom is open to all—even the outcasts and the rejected people of the world. His love is available. The doors are open, the table is set, and God is looking forward to your company.

> *For Christ died for sins once for all, the righteous for the unrighteous, to bring you to God.*   *(1 Peter 3:18)*

TOPICS: Distractions, excuses, God's character, God's kingdom, Pharisees, priorities, witnessing

MEMORY SPARKS: To find yourself in this story, think of a time when . . .
1. You were invited somewhere but didn't go because you had something else you wanted to do . . . and then later, you regretted your choice . . .
2. You made up an excuse so you could do your own thing rather than God's . . .
3. You asked someone out and she (or he) made up a lame excuse as a way of saying no . . .

To help your students connect with this story, say, "Think of a time when . . ."
1. You made up an excuse to get out of something you didn't want to do . . .
2. Everyone seemed to have more important things to do than spend time with you . . .
3. You invited a lot of people to something and only a few came . . .

HERE'S WHAT'S GOING ON:

Jesus and the Pharisees didn't see eye-to-eye. The Pharisees were often on the prowl to try and catch him saying or doing something that they could use against him. They didn't like the fact that the people followed him, respected him, honored him, and enjoyed listening to him. Jesus was a threat to their power. They especially didn't like that.

So, one night, a prominent Pharisee invited Jesus over for dinner on a Sabbath day (the day set aside for rest and worship). They were all keeping an eye on Jesus, especially when a guy with an edema (some translations call it "dropsy") showed up, hoping to be healed.

Jesus didn't skirt the issue. He asked them if they considered it against the law to heal on the Sabbath. Of course, they didn't want to say yes because they'd seem heartless and insensitive. And they didn't want to say no because then they'd be giving their approval to Jesus! So they didn't say anything.

Well, Jesus healed the man and sent him on his way. But he didn't drop the issue. He said to the Pharisees,

> *"If one of you has a son or an ox that falls into a well on the Sabbath day, will you not immediately pull him out?" And they had nothing to say.*   *(Luke 14:5, 6)*

---

[1] This story is similar to the story Jesus told in Matthew 22:1-14. However, the stories differ in a number of significant ways; so I believe they were two different parables, rather than versions of the same story. For that reason, I've referred only to Luke 14:16-24 in this chapter.

Jesus points out that any fair-minded person would help his son (or even his ox!) out of a well, no matter what day it was. Compassion doesn't take time off.

QuickTip #24 - Prepare to Be Spontaneous!

The best storytellers are able to effortlessly combine preparation with responsiveness. Rather than just plugging away at the story the way they may have practiced it, they're spontaneous enough to ad-lib or change the wording on the spot if it'll better reach their listeners.

So, as you tell your stories, pay attention to what's happening in the room. Don't worry about how the story is supposed to go or how it went in rehearsal.

Instead, be aware of what's happening. Then work at combining preparation with spontaneity to improve the excellence of your story delivery.

But once again, they don't want to get caught agreeing with Jesus, so they're silent.

Then Jesus takes a few minutes to point out the practical advantages of humility. He directs his story to the people whom he noticed were vying for the places of honor at the banquet. Finally, Jesus turns to the host of the meal and says that, rather than inviting those who might one day repay you for your kindness or dinner invitation, you should go out of your way to invite those who have no means of repaying you—*"But when you give a banquet, invite the poor, the crippled, the lame, the blind, and you will be blessed. Although they cannot repay you, you will be repaid at the resurrection of the righteous" (Luke 14:13, 14).*

Jesus' words must have had some impact because, at that point, one of the guests was so impressed that he gushed, *"Blessed is the man who will eat at the feast in the kingdom of God" (Luke 14:15).*

It was on the heels of this comment that Jesus told his story.

Here's What the Story's About:

Keep in mind all of Jesus' talk about feasts and humility and undeserving people being invited to parties. All of these images set the stage for his story.

A man was preparing a great feast. He'd sent out invitations, and now, according to tradition, he sent a messenger to tell everyone it was time for the party to begin.

But the folks who'd been invited began to make excuses, one by one.

"I bought a field, sight unseen. I need to go and check it out. Sorry, I can't make it."

Another guy said, "Yeah, and I bought some oxen and haven't tried 'em out yet. I need to head to the fields."

"So sorry!" said a third guy. "When I accepted your invitation, I forgot I was gonna get married today. I'm off to my honeymoon. See ya later!"

Obviously, the guy who'd planned the party wasn't happy. Each of his guests was blowing him off. So he sent his servant out to invite *"the poor, the crippled, the blind and the lame" (Luke 14:31).*

Only then does he find out his thoughtful servant has already done that. But still, there's room at the party. The host sends him out one last time: "Gather anyone who will come. There's room at my table! I'm throwing a party, and if the ones I invited first won't come, then I'll invite others!"

There's still room at the table. There's still room at the party. There's still room in the kingdom of God. That's the message you want your students to get from this story.

God's invitation is for real. He has a party planned, and he doesn't want to attend it alone. Feasting at the kingdom of God is a blessing that's been offered to us all.

Don't put off placing your faith in him. Don't turn him down. Accept the invitation to come to the party!

QuickTip #25 - See the Three!

This is another story that incorporates "the pattern of three." Three people make up three different excuses, three times the servant is sent out, and three different groups of people are mentioned (the "many guests," the "poor, the crippled, the blind and the lame," and the final group of people by the "roads and lanes").

TELLING THIS STORY TO STUDENTS AGES 3-7

You may wish to begin your lesson by telling or reading the following **fable**.

Leonardo the Lion was the King of All the Animals. His friends, Tessa the Tiger and Jasmine the Jaguar, were resting by his side.

"Tessa, I'm planning to throw a party!" said Leonardo. "A great party! Go and invite the other animals to come!"

So Tessa bounded off and invited Spunky the Squirrel, Mitzy the Mouse, George the Wolf, and the rest of the forest friends.

They all agreed to come.

"Cool!" said George. "I love parties!"

Leonardo prepared everything. He and Jasmine laid lots of large green leaves on the ground with berries, nuts, and seeds for the little animals to eat . . . cabbage and carrots for the rabbits . . . and a large meaty bone for George the Wolf.

"Cool!" said George. "I love bones!"

After everything was ready, Leonardo sent Tessa to tell all the animals it was time to come. But when she went to call them, they each made up different excuses for not coming!

"I'm nibbling a hole," said Mitzy the Mouse.

"I'm busy burying nuts," said Spunky the Squirrel.

"And I've gotta go howl," said George. "Cool! I love howling!"

So Tessa returned to Leonardo and told him all about it. He was not happy.

"Then go and invite all the animals that live in the desert," he growled, "and those from the mountains, and even those from . . . the swamp!"

"I have, Your Majesty. They're coming. But we still have more room."

"Then go and invite anyone who will come—even the mosquitoes!"

And so, all the animals who had made up excuses missed out. But all the animals who did come had a wonderful time dining with the King of All the Animals.

The end.

After telling this story say, **"Did you know that God has a big party planned? He wants all of us to come! What do you think? Should we say no thanks to God? Or should we say yes to him?"**

Then, retell Jesus' story through **organic storytelling** with creative dramatics. With this technique, you incorporate the suggestions of the audience into your story.

Included below is a sample of how this story might sound! (Notice the repetition in the story? That will help engage your younger listeners!)

A rich man wanted to throw a great big party! What did he do to get ready for the party? . . . Right! He blew up balloons! Let's all blow up some balloons . . . What else did he do? . . . Right! He set the table . . . and mixed up a cake . . . and baked it . . . and ate it up—oh yeah, we can't do that until we invite everyone over!

The rich man told one of his workers, "Go tell my friends the party is ready to start!" So the man hurried . . . Pretend you're that man, and you're walking to go get the friends . . . walk faster . . . and faster . . . run! . . . And STOP. Freeze!

Good!

Now, say this with me, "The party is ready, so come with me!" Let's say it together, "THE PARTY IS READY, SO COME WITH ME!"

But the first man shook his head no . . . he made up an excuse . . . what excuses do you think he used? . . . *(allow a few children to respond)* Those are all good ideas! In Jesus' story, the man said he had to go look at a field . . . Bad excuse! BORING! Show me two thumbs-down . . .

So the worker hurried to the next man . . . walk faster . . . faster . . . faster! And . . . STOP! Freeze!

Again he said, "The party is ready, so come with me!" Let's say it: "THE PARTY IS READY, SO COME WITH ME!"

But this guy shook his head no too! . . . he made up an excuse . . . what do you think HE might have said? . . . *(allow a few children to respond)* In Jesus' story, he said he had to go try out some oxen he just bought! . . . Bad excuse! BORING! Show me two thumbs-down . . .

He went up to the third guy! Ready? Fast . . . faster . . . faster! STOP! Freeze! He said the same thing. Ready? "THE PARTY IS READY, SO COME WITH ME!" This guy said, "I gotta go kiss my girlfriend!" . . . Bad excuse! YUCK! Show me two thumbs-down . . .

So he invited other people! Who wants to go to the party? Raise your hands! And the rich man invited some people to come who were poor, or sick, or couldn't walk!

God wants everyone in his kingdom, so don't say no to God! Say yes to God instead! The end!

	Creative Connection Section	
Field Trip Ideas	A banquet hall, a party room at a local kid-friendly restaurant, or a homeless shelter.	
Mood and Atmosphere	A festive party!	
Sensory Connections	Sight	Set the tables in the classroom with tablecloths, plates, napkins, silverware, drinks, snacks, and noisemakers (if you dare!). Include invitation cards on each plate! Balloons are always popular with kids too!
	Touch	In addition to decorative table settings, other objects that relate to the story include: a plastic cow, a deed for land, a wedding ring, food (see **Taste** section) and printed invitations. Hide your props in a kitchen drawer, and then pull them out as you tell the story!
	Hearing	Tractor sounds, oxen sounds, wedding music, party (or dance) music!
	Taste	This story is about a banquet or a feast (in kid-language, "a party!"). So have kid-friendly snacks to feast on and let your imagination (and your taste buds) soar! For a great confection connection, serve some candy!
	Smell	Think "party" here! Any fresh bakery items or even hot dogs will do the trick!
Costume Ideas	Dress up like a waiter at a fancy restaurant, with a towel hanging over your arm and everything!	

TELLING THIS STORY TO STUDENTS AGES 8-12

To introduce this story, you may wish to ask the children where they would like to go if they were holding a party. What restaurant would they visit? What types of food would they eat? How would they feel if they planned the party, and none of their friends showed up? Then tell or read the following **contemporary retelling** of Jesus' story.

Feast for the Least
(a contemporary retelling of "The Great Banquet")

Once, there was a kid named Joey. He lived on the edge of New York City near a hospital, where his mom worked with kids who had cancer. One day, Joey sent out 30 invitations for all his friends to come to his birthday party. All the kids said, "Sure, sounds awesome. I'll be there."

"Cool!" said Joey.

So then, Joey and his mom went shopping. They bought cake and ice cream and lots and lots of pizza. They bought cool treat bags for everyone. They spent a fortune!

"Is it too expensive to get all this stuff?" asked Joey.

"Naw, it's OK," said Joey's mom. "It's for your friends."

And then, the day of the party arrived. Joey was so excited! He thought it was gonna be the best party of the year!

The party was supposed to start at 5:00 that evening.

At 4:30, Joey walked around the house making sure everything was ready. He could smell the cake. He could almost taste it!

Then, at quarter to five, he went to sit by the window to watch for his friends.

He watched and watched.

The driveway was empty.

Five minutes 'til five. Still no one there.

He opened the door and peeked outside to see if they were coming down the street. Nope. No one. Not one.

Five o'clock came and went and no one showed up.

"Where is everybody?" Joey asked his mom.

"I don't know," she said. "I'll call their moms and find out if they're on the way."

So Joey's mom called Reggie Jefferson's mom. "Hey! We're all set to start the party!" she said. "Do you need directions to our house?"

"Um . . . we're not gonna be able to make it," she said. "Tonight's the night we clip Reggie's toenails. We'll be busy the whole time. Sorry."

Those are some long toenails, thought Joey's mom. So she called up the next person. And the next. And the next. But each of the kids and each of the parents she talked to had another excuse . . . we gotta clean the iguana's water bowl . . . we bought a new computer last month and we need to install some outdated software . . . we need to wax the toilets tonight, sorry . . ."

Every excuse was more lame than the one before!

"But it's Friday night! It's time for the party!" she said. But none of them would come.

"Are my friends coming over?" asked Joey.

"Um . . . no," said his mother. "I'm so sorry. They're not coming."

"None of 'em?"

"No. None of 'em."

Now, most kids might be sad at a time like that. Most kids might wonder if their friends really liked 'em or not. Most kids, maybe. But not Joey. He got mad! After all, they'd told him earlier they were gonna come!

"Well, Mom, you know what I think we should do? I think we should take all this food to the kids you work with at the hospital and give it to them. After all, they only have junky hospital food to eat. I'll have my party there!"

Joey's mom smiled. "That's a great idea. But I think we're still gonna have extra food. We really bought a lot!"

I'll say, thought Joey.

"Then we'll give some to the people we meet on the way . . . none of those people we invited at first are gonna get a taste of this food."

And so all of Joey's friends missed out.

And Joey and his mom took the party to people who would appreciate it.

And believe me, they did.

The end.

Compare the story of Joey with Jesus' parable. Discuss the application of Jesus' story for us today:

1. What kind of excuses did Joey's friends make? Did they have good reasons?
2. What kind of excuses do people give God today?
3. What excuses have you used with God?
4. How do you think that makes God feel?
5. What do you need to tell God right now?

You could tell the following version of Jesus' story by yourself or with a partner. When two storytellers tell a story together, alternating speaking parts, it's called **tandem storytelling**.

Tandem stories can also be used as puppet scripts! If you use this story as a **puppet script,** you'll need to make sure you have a good way for the puppets to cue the audience on when to say their parts.

Party Favorites
(a tandem storytelling/signal cards version of "The Great Banquet")

Notes for the storytellers: Here are your options: you could hold up appropriate objects, such as a party hat (for the cheering) and a plunger (for the groaning), or you could draw a smiley face and a frowny face on a piece of poster board. Or you could simply cue the audience on when to say their parts by pausing and gesturing toward them with a big thumbs-up or thumbs-down! (Cue words for these actions are underlined.)

Be aware that some of the older kids may want to say the wrong thing on purpose, just to get attention. Don't encourage them, or they'll get carried away messing up the story and distract the other children.

(The story is written for two storytellers with references to "we" and "us." If you tell the story yourself, you'll want to edit the story slightly and change those references to "I" and "me.")

BONNIE: **Kids, today we're gonna need your help!**

GEORGE: **Whenever we hold up this sign** *(or hat, or picture)*, **we want you to cheer by yelling, "Yeah!" Let's try it!** *(hold it up and let them respond)* **Great job!**

BONNIE: **And whenever we hold up this sign** *(or plunger, or picture)*, **we want you to groan and say, "Aw . . ."** **Let's practice that!**

(hold it up and let them respond) **Pay close attention! You only get to say it when we hold up the sign!** *(or plunger, or picture)*

GEORGE: **Once there was a man who decided to throw a great big party!** *(hold up the "Yeah!" sign or object and let them cheer!)*

BONNIE: **So he invited lots of his friends. And they all said, "Cool! We'd love to come to your party!** *("Yeah!" sign)*

GEORGE: So he got everything ready.

BONNIE: Then, he sent out one of his servants to go and gather the people . . .

GEORGE: *(with rhythm)* **The table's set! The food is hot! The soup is simmerin' in the pot! The time has come! The party's here! With lotsa food and cold root beer!**
("Yeah!" sign)

BONNIE: **Um . . . I don't think he rapped it . . .**

GEORGE: **Too bad . . .** *("Aw . . ." sign)*

BONNIE: **But when the servant arrived, the people began to make excuses!**
("Aw . . ." sign)

GEORGE: **Sorry, I just bought a field and need to go see it.**

BONNIE: **But what about the party?!**
("Yeah!" sign)

GEORGE: **Maybe next time.**
("Aw . . ." sign)

BONNIE: **So, he didn't come. And the second guy made another excuse . . .** *("Aw . . ." sign)*

GEORGE: **I just bought an Xbox* and haven't tried it out yet.**
("Aw . . ." sign)

BONNIE: **Um . . . in the story he doesn't buy an Xbox, he buys five oxen.**

GEORGE: **Oh, sorry. I just bought five Xboxes!** *("Yeah!" sign)*

BONNIE: **Oxen, not boxes!**

GEORGE: **Oh, five Xboxen . . .**

BONNIE: **. . . Oh, brother—**

GEORGE: **—and I have to go try all five of 'em out!** *("Yeah!" sign)*

BONNIE: **Close enough. He did go to try out his oxen and missed the party. And another guy said he'd just gotten married and had to go see his wife.**

GEORGE: *("Aw . . ." sign)* **I mean . . .**
("Yeah!" sign)

BONNIE: **So all of them refused to come. They all made excuses.**
("Aw . . ." sign)

GEORGE: **So the servant returned to his master.**

BONNIE: **And the master got angry.**

GEORGE: *(as the master)* **"Go out and invite other people to come! Invite people who are sick, or poor, or blind, or disabled! We'll enjoy the party with them!"**
("Yeah!" sign) **Because . . .** *(with rhythm)* **the table's set! The food is hot! The soup is simmerin' in the pot! The time has come! The party's here! With lotsa food and cold root beer!**
("Yeah!" sign)

BONNIE: **But the servant told him he'd already invited all those people too! And there was STILL more room!**

GEORGE: *(as the master)* **"Then go out and make 'em come in! Bring anyone you can find wandering around on the roads. Homeless people, bums, robbers, I don't care. Bring 'em all in until my house is full! None of those people I invited before are gonna be able to enjoy this food!** *("Aw . . ." sign)* **But as for the rest of us—to everyone who'll come—we're gonna party!** *("Yeah!" sign)*

TOGETHER: **The end!** *(Optional . . . "Aw . . ." sign)*

(Bow. Fade out the stage lights as the storytellers exit.)

Xbox® is a registered trademark of Microsoft.

The Great Banquet 73

When the story is finished, transition by saying something like, **"That's a story about God's kingdom! If we don't accept his invitation, we're never gonna be able to join the party in Heaven and live happily ever after with him! But if we say yes to God, we can be with him in Heaven forever!"**

W.E.G.I. (Weird & Extremely Goofy Ideas)

Since this story happens at a party, playing games with food might be lots of fun! Here are a couple of wacky ideas to get you started:

Spam® Lunchmeat games - (1) Meat Tag - The ITs each carry a slab of lunchmeat and use it to tag folks. (2) Meat Toss - Forget the old "egg toss" standby. Try tossing lunchmeat. Or gelatin. Or tomatoes.

Blow up some party balloons and draw smiley faces on them with permanent markers. Then, have contests to see who can shave them! Use real razors and shaving cream. When the balloons explode, shaving cream flies all over!

PRAYER CONNECTION:
1. Pray for the humility to accept God's invitation.
2. Pray for all those who have rejected God or put him off until later.
3. Pray for opportunities to invite others into the kingdom of Heaven.

INTERACTIVE PRAYER IDEA:
Join together in a responsive reading of Psalm 9:1, 2. Read the verses, and after every line, have the children respond by saying to God, **"I will say yes to you!"**

> *I will praise you, O LORD, with all my heart;*
> I WILL SAY YES TO YOU!
>
> *I will tell of all your wonders.*
> I WILL SAY YES TO YOU!
>
> *I will be glad and rejoice in you;*
> I WILL SAY YES TO YOU!
>
> *I will sing praise to your name, O Most High.*
> I WILL SAY YES TO YOU!

Then, hand out party hats, noisemakers, or birthday candles. Tell the children to carry the party items around. **"And if anyone asks you if you were at a party, tell 'em, 'No, but I'm gonna be!' And then tell 'em today's story!"**

Lost and Found (Three Stories in One!) 8

BASED ON: Luke 15[1]

BIG IDEA: God can't help but celebrate when lost souls are found.

GRACE CONNECTION: God is in the business of seeking, finding, and celebrating. That's what lies at the heart of God's character. We're all lost. We all need to be found. And he is seeking us. That's why God parties every time a sinner repents. As Jesus said:

> *And I, the Son of Man, have come to seek and save those like him who are lost.*   *(Luke 19:10, NLT)*

TOPICS: Faith, forgiveness, God's character, God's kingdom, grace, Pharisees, repentance, sin

MEMORY SPARKS FOR "THE LOST SHEEP" (LUKE 15:3-7):

In this story, Jesus emphasizes being lost, being found, caring enough to seek the lost, and celebration. To find yourself in this story, think of a time when . . .

1. You wandered from God . . . How did it feel? What happened?
2. God found you and carried you home . . .
3. You joined the homecoming party . . . (like the friends)

To help your students connect with this story, say, "Think of a time when . . ."

1. You waited for someone to stop being mean and to say he was sorry . . . (like the other sheep)
2. You lost a pet dog or cat and went looking for it . . . (like the shepherd)
3. You got lost in a store or a mall and couldn't find your parents . . . (like the sheep)

MEMORY SPARKS FOR "THE LOST COIN" (LUKE 15:8-10):

In this story, Jesus emphasizes the value of the lost item, dedication to the search, and celebration. To find yourself in this story, think of a time when . . . you lost your car keys and needed to find them pronto . . . How hard did you search? Why?

To help your students connect with this story, say, "Think of a time when you found something important that had been lost for a long time. . . ."

MEMORY SPARKS FOR "THE LOST SONS" (LUKE 15:11-32):

In this story, Jesus emphasizes rebellion and restoration (younger son), love and forgiveness (father), bitterness and resentment (older son), and, once again, celebration.

To find yourself in this story, think of a time when . . .

1. You were jealous of the attention or promotion given to someone else . . .
2. You finally returned home and found God's arms open wide . . .
3. You said you were sorry just so you wouldn't get into trouble . . .

To help your students connect with this story, say, "Think of a time when . . ."

1. Your parents did something special for a brother or sister . . . Were you jealous or joyful? Why? What happened?
2. You apologized for something, not because you were sorry, but because you wanted to get something out of it . . .
3. You thought your dad was gonna say, "I told you so!" but he didn't. He just forgave you instead . . .

[1] In Luke 15, Jesus told the parables of "The Lost Sheep," "The Lost Coin," and "The Lost Sons" (otherwise known as "The Prodigal Son"). Some people separate them into three stories, but I believe that, taken in context, they form one complete story. For that reason, I've included them all together in one chapter.

Here's What's Going On:

The religious leaders were familiar with Jesus' ways. They'd seen who he preferred to hang out with—the "sinners" (see Luke 15:1). Actually, since all of us are sinners, their mutterings about "sinners" reveal an awful lot about their attitude. They didn't think they were sinners—just that other people were, like prostitutes and thieves.

In response to their mumbling, Jesus told his story of being lost and found.[2]

By the way, this story is extremely relevant today. Most church people today don't party with prostitutes and thieves any more than the Pharisees did. But Jesus did. In his perfect love, he never justified sinful behavior, but he never let the lost feel unwelcomed either. People today tend to do one or the other (either point out the truth or love the lost), but they rarely do both.

Some people want to be "tolerant," so they create "relevant," inviting churches that don't stand up for God's Word because they're afraid the truth might offend someone.

Other people, in their quest to teach and preach the truth, become judgmental, legalistic, and unloving. Take a close look at your church or denomination and you'll probably see where it lies on the continuum.

We need to model a more Christlike attitude and lifestyle. As extensions of Christ's body, it's the job of all believers to make the church the most inviting and loving place on earth—the place where notorious sinners feel more welcomed and loved than they would at a bar, a nightclub, a casino, or a ball game—and to still uphold the truth. This mixture of love and justice, of grace and truth, is what the gospel is all about.

> *Instead, speaking the truth in love, we will in all things grow up into him who is the Head, that is, Christ.* (Ephesians 4:15)

Here's What the Story's About:

This chapter of the Bible is really a treasure trove of three of Jesus' most beloved and timeless parables.[3]

Jesus weaves his stories together with his refrain: *"There will be rejoicing in heaven over one sinner who repents."* He says this after each of the first two stories, and then shows it happening in the third story (see Luke 15:7, 10, 32).

It's significant to note that Jesus leaves the story of "The Lost Sons" unfinished. We never find out if the older brother enters the party or not. Remember who Jesus' audience is? In Luke 15:1 we find out that Jesus is talking to the judgmental Pharisees:

> *Now the tax collectors and "sinners" were all gathering around to hear him. But the Pharisees and the teachers of the law muttered, "This man welcomes sinners and eats with them." Then Jesus told them this parable . . .* (Luke 15:1-3)

With this audience in mind, it makes sense that Jesus ends the story without resolving the question of whether or not the older brother enters the party. Because, now that he has answered their question about why he eats with sinners (see Luke 15:32), the question still remains as to whether or not they will repent and enter the party.

QuickTip #26 - Use Stories from All of L.I.F.E.!

In order to present an entire program based on one Bible story, consider telling other stories that relate to the same themes. Think about stories from your own **L.I.F.E**—**L**iterature (stories you've read), **I**magination (stories you've made up), **F**olklore (stories you've heard), and **E**xperience (memories you have).

When doing this, it's often most effective to tell the Bible story last so that the rest of the stories all point toward it.

---

[2] Some commentators have noted that Luke 15:3 says Jesus told them "this parable," not "these parables." They contend that the parables in this chapter really combine to form one complete story. They make a good point: the three short stories are all interconnected and form a more complete picture of God's grace when studied together.

[3] There's another version of "The Lost Sheep" story recorded in Matthew 18:12-14. There Jesus emphasized God's specific and individual love for children.

Telling This Story to Students Ages 3-7

There are a lot of parties in this story! To help your students think about the mood of parties, you might wish to introduce Jesus' story by saying, **"Picture with me a 6-year-old's birthday party . . . What's going on? . . . What games are they playing? . . . What kind of cake do you think they have? . . . What other food is there? . . . Are there any presents? What do you think they are? . . ."**

Explain that God is into parties! In fact, that was Jesus' favorite thing to compare Heaven to!

Come Out! Come Out! Wherever You Are!
(a game about being lost and found)

Play a game of hide-and-seek. Then ask, **"Would it be fun if you were playing hide-and-seek and no one ever came looking for you? Of course not! It would get lonely! Well, in a certain way, we're all hiding from God. We've all done things that make God sad. And, rather than say we're sorry, usually people just try to get away with it.**

"But God comes looking for us so that he can forgive us. Today we're gonna talk about some things that were lost and found to remind us that God wants to find us, forgive us, and welcome us into Heaven!"

Discuss ways that people are lost or ways that we hide from God. You may wish to review the story of Adam and Eve hiding from God in the Garden of Eden. How is that story similar to this story? How is it different? How is God's grace evident in both stories?

Listed below is a **sound effects** story. With this technique, one storyteller retells the story while a helper (or helpers) makes sound effects (teenage volunteers would be great at this!). You can let the sound effects person make up his own sounds, or use the ones suggested below.

It's ideal to let the sound effects person have a microphone so that it's easy for the listeners to hear him. If desired, you could also have the entire class make the sound effects rather than just one person!

The Kind Shepherd
(a sound effects version of "The Lost Sheep")

What to say:	Suggested sound effects:
A shepherd was a man who watched over a lot of sheep. Sometimes they would *baa!* all night long . . .	Baa.
Sometimes they would fall asleep and snore really loudly . . .	(Snore)
. . . other times they would slurp water from the stream . . .	(Slurp)
. . . or munch on the grass in the field . . .	(Munch)
And sometimes they would wander off and bump into boulders!	Ouch!
The shepherd kept 'em up in the mountains where he protected them from howling wolves . . .	(Howl)
. . . and angry bears . . .	(Growl)
. . . and pokey porcupines . . .	Ouch!
One day, as he was counting his sheep . . .	1, 2, 3, 4 . . .
He noticed that one was missing!	Uh-oh.
He counted again . . .	1, 2, 3, 4 . . .
. . . and again . . .	1, 2, 3, 4 . . .

. . . and again . . .	1, 2, 3, 4 . . .
. . . to make sure. But it was true! One sheep was gone!	Uh-oh!
So he left the other sheep out there, munching on the grass.	(Munch)
And he went off in search of his lost sheep . . .	"He-e-e-re, Sheepy, sheepy, sheepy, sheepy!"
He looked up on the cold, windy mountaintop . . .	Whoosh. Whoosh.
. . . and in dark, damp, spooky caves . . .	O-o-o-o-o-o-oh!
. . . and in tall, swishing grass . . .	Swish. Swish.
. . . where there were snakes!	Sss! Sss!
. . . and mice . . .	Squeak! Squeak!
. . . and snakes chasing mice . . .	Sss! Squeak! Sss! Squeak!
Soon he got tired and fell asleep, snoring even louder than those sheep did!	(SNORE)
When suddenly, he woke up, and there was his sheep munching on some grass!	(Munch)
He was excited!	*(singing)* Hallelujah! Hallelujah!
He put it on his shoulders. But the sheep was pretty fat, so he grunted . . .	Oof. (Grunt)
I mean, he grunted a whole lot on the way home . . .	(Grunt. Grunt. Grunt.)
And when he got home, he invited all his friends over for a party to celebrate!	(Cheer! Get funky!)
The end.	*(singing)* Hallelujah! Hallelujah!

Another creative storytelling technique that's popular with younger children is **organic storytelling**. When you tell organic stories, begin with the framework of the story, and then add details based on suggestions given by your listeners. Obviously, your version will be somewhat different than the one on the following page because it'll depend on the specific suggestions of your students. (Underlined words indicate responses that will change per your students' suggestions. Be ready for them to suggest some unusual places to search, such as a swimming pool, an airport, or even a toilet!)

Kids, today's Bible story is about a woman who lost her coin. It was very precious to her, and she wanted to find it really badly.

Let's act out the story as I tell it!

Now, if you were a lady who lost your coin, where might you look for it? *(allow them to respond)* That's right! You'd look in a drawer! Let's pretend to look in a drawer . . . It's dark in there! Feel around. Is the coin there? Hm . . . where could it be?

Where else would you look? *(allow them to respond).* Right! You'd look under your bed! Bend over and look . . . Push the big dust balls out of the way . . . Good . . . No coin here though . . . Hm . . . Where else? *(allow them to respond)* . . .

OK! Let's all look in the yard! Push the tall grass out of the way . . . Watch out for rocks, don't stub your toe! . . . Ouch! . . .

(invite more suggestions if you wish, end by finding the coin)

Look! There's the coin! Pick it up! Let's go back inside and have a party with our friends to celebrate! As Jesus said, *"In the same way, I tell you, there is rejoicing in the presence of the angels of God over one sinner who repents" (Luke 15:10).*

Discuss what it means to repent and to believe in Jesus.

The Parable of the Forgiving Father
(a storymime of "The Lost Sons")

Notes for the storyteller: As you and a partner lead this story, one of you reads or says the words while the other person leads the actions. As each action is performed, the audience mirrors the action back to you. Practice this story a few times before performing it to make sure the pace is smooth and the pauses are long enough. Photocopy this story so you each have a copy to read from.

What to say:	What to do:
Once there was a father who had two sons . . .	Hold up 2 fingers.
They grew from babies . . .	Suck your thumb like a baby.
. . . into young men . . .	Flex your muscles.
One day, the younger one decided to leave home.	Wave good-bye to someone.
He got money from his dad	Hold out your hand and pretend to weigh gold coins in your hand.
. . . and took off.	Turn sideways and walk in place.
He went far away—over land . . .	Drive a steering wheel. Honk the horn.
. . . and sea . . .	Make ocean waves with your hands.
Alright, well, maybe not over sea . . .	Drive your steering wheel again.
But, finally, he came to The Big City . . .	Look way up, as if seeing a giant! "Whoa, mama!"
And he had good times there, eating . . .	Shovel food into your mouth.
. . . and drinking . . .	Guzzle cans of soda.
. . . and partying with his new friends . . .	Dance around and get funky.
But soon, all his money was gone . . .	Turn your pants pockets inside out. "Uh-oh."
So he started working on a pig farm . . .	Hold your nose as if you're smelling a pig farm. "Whoa, baby!"
. . . feeding the pigs!	Toss slop. "Gross!"
One day he realized how hungry he was . . .	Rub your tummy. "Be still, my aching belly."
And he decided to go back home.	Turn sideways and walk in place.
His dad saw him coming!	Put your hand above your eyes *(or make binoculars).* "Cool!"
And ran out to meet him.	Run in place.
The dad hugged his son.	Hug someone. "I love you, son!"
And they had a good time, eating . . .	Shovel food into your mouth.
. . . and drinking . . .	Guzzle cans of soda.

. . . and partying together . . .	Dance around and get funky.
But then, the older brother came home from work.	Fold your arms across your chest.
And he wouldn't join the party.	Hold up a hand like you're stopping traffic and shake your head no.
Even when his father invited him in.	Gesture to the crowd to come toward you. "Come in."
He just stood there, all angry because he didn't think his dad was being fair.	Fold your arms across your chest. "Humph!"
So, finally, his father went back in to the party,	Shrug your shoulders
And the older brother just stood there all alone on the porch	Fold your arms across your chest.
While everyone at the party had a great time, eating . . .	Shovel food into your mouth.
and drinking . . .	Guzzle cans of soda.
. . . and partying together . . .	Dance around and get REALLY funky.

(say these lines together)
For God's kingdom is waiting, the door's open WIDE.
So, will you stay on the porch, or come on INSIDE?

The end.	Take a bow.

Note that this ending gets at the heart of Jesus' parable to the Pharisees. Also note the repetition. This helps students remember the story and anticipate their part!

Discuss the three stories and close in prayer.

QuickTip #27 - Model the Master!
Anytime you put together a whole lesson, look for ways to tell stories that all relate to the same point, or restate the same theme in a slightly different way. Then weave them together by including a simple refrain between them. That's exactly what Jesus did in Luke 15!

		Creative Connection Section [4]
Field Trip Ideas		Lost Sheep - Tell the story in a field. Lost Coin - Tell the story in a broom closet. Lost Sons - Tell the story in a living room, dance club, or roller skating rink (to emphasize the dancing and celebration!).
Mood and Atmosphere		Lost Sheep - dedication, longing, celebration. Lost Coin - frustration, diligence, celebration. Lost Sons - arrogance, humiliation, love, resentment, pride.
Sensory Connections	Sight	You may wish to have a scavenger hunt to search for wool . . . coins . . . candles . . . brooms . . . and other items from the story.
	Touch	Hold up or hand around objects that relate to the story. For "The Lost Coin" story, pull your props out of a purse!
	Hearing	Lots of sounds accompany these stories: the *baa*ing of sheep . . . the *swish*ing of a broom . . . the grunting of pigs . . . the sound of parties! Weave them in!
	Taste	There's a party in each of these stories. So serve food you'd typically have at a party. When someone trusts in Jesus, it's his spiritual birthday. If you have someone in your class who has recently become a Christian, throw him a spiritual birthday party!
	Smell	From pig farms to roast beef, the story of "The Lost Sons" is full of smells! Consider having a *smell* scavenger hunt where students try to collect items that relate to any of the scenes from the three stories!
Costume Ideas		To bring unity to the stories, use a cane as your only prop and retell all three stories. Use the cane as a shepherd's staff for "The Lost Sheep," as a broom for "The Lost Coin," and then as a cane for the father in "The Lost Sons"!

TELLING THIS STORY TO STUDENTS AGES 8-12

Many older students have heard these stories before, so it's fun to retell them in fresh and unexpected ways!

[4] For 80 more creative drama, writing, craft, prayer, and life application ideas for the story of "The Lost Sons," see pages 103–109 in my book *The Creative Storytelling Guide for Children's Ministry* (2002, Standard Publishing).

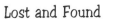

Hide and Go Sheep!

(a fill-in version of "The Lost Sheep")

Notes for the storyteller: When you tell a **fill-in** story, DON'T REVEAL WHICH STORY YOU'RE STUDYING. Instead, simply begin by gathering suggestions from the audience and writing the words on the blanks within the story. Encourage the kids to say words that are a little unusual!

(Be aware that sometimes you may need to change the form or case of a word. For example, they may say *bunny* and you need to change it to *bunnies* as you read the story aloud. Just be aware of the flow of the story, and you should be fine!)

When you're done, review the Bible story to see how close to (or far away from) your version it was!

This is the parable of "The Lost Sheep" . . .

Long ago Jesus told this story . . .

Once there was a shepherd. It was his job to watch over all the _____.
                                                                              (an unusual animal, plural)

He stayed up in the hills making sure that they were safe from _____, and
                                                                    (another unusual animal)

from ferocious, bloodthirsty, killer _____.
                                        (a cute, furry, little animal)

Every day he was careful to make sure his animals never _____.
                                                              (something you should not do)

One day he was counting his flock. Now, usually he was supposed to have

_____ but this day he realized he only had_____.

(a number between 1 and a million)   *(one less than the number you just said)*

And he said, "_____! I've lost one of my _____!"

             (a weird saying)   *(the animal he's watching)*

So the shepherd left the rest of the flock and searched for the missing animal. He searched all over! I mean, he looked in every place he could think of, from _____, to

                                                                              (a place far away)

_____. He searched in mountains and in deep, dark, scary caves filled with

(a place nearby)

_____.

(something disgusting)

Finally, he found his lost _____!

                              (the animal he's watching)

"Hurray!" said the shepherd.

"_____!" said the _____.

   (an animal sound)   *(the animal he's watching)*

He put it on his _____ and hurried home.

                      (a body part)

When he got home, he called up all of his friends and said, "_____!

                                                              (something cool people say all the time)

I've found my lost _____!"

                        (the animal he's watching)

"_____!" said his friends. "Let's party until _____!"

(something teenage girls say)   *(a day sometime in the future)*

In the same way, there's a party in Heaven every time a sinner repents. The end.

When you tell stories to preteens, it's fun to use unusual **props** or tell familiar stories in unique and memorable ways. They especially enjoy it when things get a little goofy, like they do in this next story!

Flamethrower Barbie*
(a prop-intensive, W.E.G.I. version of "The Lost Coin")

Notes for the storyteller: Consider making this story into a homemade video that you can show your students in class! To include all the ideas in the script, you'll need:

- a Barbie doll
- a hamster cage (optional)
- a toy vacuum cleaner
- a fish bowl
- extra Barbie clothes
- a hand-vac
- a cell phone
- a trigger-operated butane lighter
- extra dolls

What to say:	What to do:
Once there was a woman who lost a coin . . .	Pull out your Barbie doll and wave her at the audience.
(say this in your best airhead voice) "Oh, my goodness, I wonder where it is?"	Whenever you speak for Barbie from now on, use the same voice . . .
She looked all over her house . . .	Make Barbie look all over, including in the ears of some of your students . . . Then say, "Nope! That's empty!"
She looked under the couch . . . "Not down there!"	Tip her upside down and swing her around . . .
She even looked in the fish bowl . . . "Nope, not there either!"	Stick her head in the fish bowl and swish her around a little bit . . .
She looked up high, by the ceiling . . .	Toss her up into the air a few times . . .
But she couldn't find her coin anywhere . . .	Make her look at the audience, and then tip her head down toward them as if she's sad . . . Make crying sounds . . .
"It must be here somewhere . . . Hmmm, where could it be?"	Bop her back and forth like she's thinking.

(If desired, insert your own additional ideas of where she searched . . . consider things like looking in the hamster cage—turn your back to the audience, stick the doll near the hamster and then say in her voice, "Ah! Let go of my head!" and rip her head off before turning back to the audience . . . use your imagination . . .)

And then, she lit a lamp to help her look . . . *(look at her and say)* "Hm . . . Flamethrower Barbie!"	Pull out a butane lighter and let her hold it . . .
Then she thought, "Maybe it's on the floor somewhere!" So she swept the house, looking for her coin . . .	Pull out a toy vacuum cleaner at first . . . and then pull out a hand-vac and have her say . . . "This oughtta do the trick!"
(if you have extra Barbie clothes, have the hand-vac suck them up) Oops.	Turn off the hand-vac and put it away.
Finally, underneath the refrigerator, she found her lost coin!	Hold up a penny.
(with rhythm as an airhead) "I have found my coin! I have found my coin! . . . Hurray, hurray, hurray, hurray! I have found my coin!"	Bop her head back and forth like she's a real airhead.
And so she called up all her friends on the phone . . .	Flip open a cell phone and hold it up to her ear.
and invited them over to a party to celebrate.	Fold up the cell phone and put it away.
And they were all, like, *(in a hip, urban girl voice)* "You go, girl! We'll be there right away!"	Pull out more dolls.

*Barbie® is a registered trademark of Mattel, Inc.

And Jesus said, "in the same way, there's rejoicing in Heaven over one sinner who repents." The end.	Make them all dance around . . . Bend her over so it looks like she's taking a bow.

When you're done, emphasize how important each one of us is to God. There are no nobodies! God is searching for you . . . Will you hide from him or let yourself be found?

Since many older students have already heard the story of "The Lost Sons," have them tell it to you as an **add-on** story!

Choose 8–10 students and explain that you're going to have them retell the story without looking in their Bibles.

The first student will begin the first part of the story. The next student will continue where the first one left off. Each student thereafter does the same. The rule is, the last person must finish up the story! Then, when you're done, compare the version the students told with the one found in the Bible! It can be hilarious to see how much the story has changed in the retelling!

Finally, here's an idea for retelling "The Lost Sons." Do the following **contemporary retelling** as is, or adapt it into a **monologue**.

Alone on the Porch [5]
(a contemporary retelling of "The Lost Sons")

Notes for the storyteller: You could use the story as is, or have two people (Jerod and a Narrator) retell it together. If you use two people, cross off any unnecessary words or phrases and have Jerod begin onstage. Set up the stage like a barbecue deck and have Jerod act out the story!

"Oh, great! Just great!" yelled Jerod Westenberg as he watched his dad walk back toward the house. "Leave me here to think it over, huh?! Well, I've already thought it over! Don't walk away from me! Do you hear me! I've made my decision. I'm gonna stay right here! DO YOU HEAR ME?!"

He watched his father disappear inside, closing the sliding patio door partway to keep out the chilly autumn air. The door stood half open.

Jerod slumped onto the deck chair next to the pool and waited. Dad would be back. He knew that. Dad would come back outside and beg him—Jerod Westenberg—to come in. Or maybe he'd feel bad and move the party outside to include him. That's the kind of softhearted guy Dad was. "So, all I gotta do is wait it out. I can outlast the old man," he reasoned. "It's just a matter of time."

He turned and glanced toward the door. He could see through the glass into the kitchen. People were getting sodas and passing around bowls of chips and nachos. A couple of pizzas lay on the counter. He could smell them from where he sat. As he stared at the house, someone turned on some music. The party was getting into full swing. Jerod shook his head as he remembered his father's words. . . . *"Are you kidding me? We gotta celebrate! Your brother is back! C'mon in, join the party!"*

He had to celebrate, huh? He had to throw a party?! A party for a loser like Ted! *Has he ever thrown a party for ME?* thought Jerod. *Not! Has he ever told ME to invite a few friends over for a barbecue? Or to watch movies or play video games? I don't think so.*

Jerod got up and began to pace back and forth beside the pool. *So that's how it's gonna be,* he said to himself. *I obey him all the time. I work hard every day. And this is the thanks I get?!*

He turned and kicked over one of those deck tables with the green and white umbrellas sticking out of the middle. It fell into the pool and slowly sank to the bottom.

From inside the house, rock music drifted out the open door. It almost sounded like they'd turned up the stereo. Unbelievable. How dare they? How dare they celebrate? It was like they were mocking him. It made him want to throw up.

[5] An earlier version of this story first appeared in my book *JawDroppers: 36 Shocking Stories for Students* (2001, Standard Publishing). Used by permission.

Jerod had always followed the rules. He never got into trouble. He got good grades. He helped out around the house. Sure, Dad would tell him to take a break sometimes, that he didn't have to put in all those extra hours, that he could take some time off and enjoy himself. Maybe join a soccer league. Or spend the weekend fishing.

But Jerod knew how things worked in the world. If you wanna get ahead, you gotta work harder than everyone else. Oh, yeah. Jerod knew. *I can earn his love. If I just work hard enough, he'll have to give me the family business when he retires. He'll owe it to me,* he would tell himself.

And now . . . there they were throwing a big homecoming celebration for his kid brother Ted. The guy who takes off for New York City to become an actor, loses everything, and shows up on their doorstep again. Penniless. Homeless. Hopeless.

Ted the actor! Yeah, no kidding. He was always acting. Pretending. Posing. Anything to get his way and get more cash from Dad. Lying. Cheating. Stealing. It didn't matter who he hurt.

And there was Dad, throwing money behind him all the way. Giving his hard-earned cash to a loser who wasted everything. "I'll pay you back, Dad, I promise," Ted would say each time he pocketed some more of Dad's dough.

Yeah, right.

Dusk settled over the neighborhood. Inside, the party was getting wilder and wilder. Jerod could see his brother and his dad slam-dancing their way through the living room. *Doesn't Dad have any dignity? He's embarrassing the whole family,* thought Jerod. *Well, he'll wise up soon enough. He'll be back out here any minute begging me to come in. He owes me that much.* Then he shouted toward the house, "Even if I have to wait here all night, I'm not coming in there! I'm not going to a party for my brother! Do you hear me?!"

But of course, with the music playing, no one did.

And so, as night began to fall, the people inside the house laughed and danced and partied on. And Jerod stood there alone on the deck with his arms folded across his chest and his teeth clenched. Staring angrily at the open door.

And no one at the party even missed him.

As a good way to review all three stories, consider having the students create **Scripture snapshots** of being lost and found. Assign groups of 4–5 children different scenes from the three stories (for example, the shepherd searching in a cave . . . the woman sweeping the floor . . . the younger brother feeding the pigs . . .). In this game students create pictures of what that scene would have looked like by positioning their bodies together into a frozen picture!

Take turns having the groups show the rest of the class their Scripture snapshots, and have everyone else try and guess which scene each is portraying. Or, line up all of the pictures and have other classes take tours of them as Tour Guides (i.e., student storytellers!) take them from one scene to the next, retelling the stories to them!

Prayer Connection:

1. Pray for those who are lost, that they might find Jesus.
2. Pray for those who look down on others, that they might learn humility.
3. Pray for those who don't know yet that they are lost, that God would reveal their sin to them.

Interactive Prayer Idea:

"Hide And Go Speak Prayers" - Everyone goes to a quiet corner of the room and says their prayers aloud, quietly, to God. Tell God you're tired of hiding from him and you want to be found.

9 Lazarus and the Rich Man

BASED ON: Luke 16:19-31

BIG IDEA: Our eternal destiny hinges upon whether or not we trust in God before we die, not on how successful or wealthy we are in this life.

GOSPEL CONNECTION: In this parable, Lazarus was saved by the grace of God through his faith. The rich man was condemned because he rejected the message of Scripture. Abraham emphasized to the rich man that it was faith, not proof, that is needed to get us into Heaven. Jesus emphasized the same thing to his disciples:

> *Whoever believes and is baptized will be saved, but whoever*
> *does not believe will be condemned.*   *(Mark 16:16)*

TOPICS: Faith, God's Word, Heaven, Hell, judgment, justice, materialism, priorities, righteousness, wealth, witnessing

MEMORY SPARKS: To find yourself in this story, think of a time when . . .
1. You discovered you weren't as close to God as you thought you were (like the rich guy at the end of the story) . . .
2. You waited and waited, and justice just didn't seem to get done (like Lazarus at the beginning of the story) . . .
3. You wondered why God doesn't just prove to everyone that he's real . . .

To help your students connect with this story, say, "Think of a time when . . ."
1. You never took the time to help someone, even though you knew you could have . . .
2. Afriends was sick, and you didn't do anything to help . . .
3. You stopped putting God first and put yourself first instead . . .

HERE'S WHAT'S GOING ON:

It's not exactly clear who the audience for this story is, but it was most likely the sneering Pharisees mentioned earlier in this chapter (in Luke 16:14). Jesus had already told one story about reprioritizing life from a more eternal perspective (see Luke 16:1-16). He summarized that earlier story this way:

> *No servant can serve two masters. Either he will hate the one and love the other,*
> *or he will be devoted to the one and despise the other. You cannot serve both God and*
> *Money.*   *(Luke 16:13)*

Here's how the Pharisees responded when Jesus said that:

> *The Pharisees, who loved money, heard all this and were sneering at Jesus. He*
> *said to them, "You are the ones who justify yourselves in the eyes of men, but God*
> *knows your hearts. What is highly valued among men is detestable in God's sight."*
> *(Luke 16:14, 15)*

Then, after a couple of additional teachings, Jesus told the story of "Lazarus and the Rich Man." And just like the story of "The Shrewd Manager" (in Luke 16:1-16), the story of "Lazarus and the Rich Man" relates to the themes of priorities, the brevity of life, and the importance of putting God first now, while we still have time.

HERE'S WHAT THE STORY'S ABOUT:

This story has a complete reversal in it. Take a moment to look at the chart below which compares Lazarus to the rich man, both in this life and in the next:

Comparing Lazarus and the Rich Man

In this life, things looked like this . . .

	THE RICH MAN	LAZARUS
Clothing	Purple clothes and fine linen	Beggar's clothes
Social status	Respected by people	Rejected by people
Comfort level	Comfortable every day	In agony every day
Income level	Rich	Poor
Housing	Lived in a nice home	Homeless (out of the house)
Physical needs	Lacked nothing	Longed for relief
Activity	Celebrated with his friends	Begged for food
Overall condition	Good	Bad

. . . but in the next life, EVERYTHING is reversed!

	THE RICH MAN	LAZARUS
Clothing	Filthy rags (see Isaiah 64:6)	Without stain or wrinkle or any blemish (see Ephesians 5:27)
Social status	Rejected by God	Respected by God
Comfort level	In agony for eternity	Comforted for eternity
Income level	Poor	Rich
Housing	Locked outside	Welcomed home (carried there by angels!)
Physical needs	Longed for relief	Lacked nothing
Activity	Begged for water	Celebrated with his Lord
Overall condition	Bad	Good

The only thing that remained the same was the inner condition of their hearts—the rich man was unrighteous, and Lazarus was righteous!

The key to Lazarus's salvation and to his righteousness is found in Abraham's last words to the rich man in Hell:

> *If they do not listen to Moses and the Prophets, they will not be convinced even if someone rises from the dead.* *(Luke 16:31)*

Our eternal destiny balances upon what we believe now, in this brief life. If we don't believe God's Word, no amount of proof (or wealth or earthly success) is going to save us.

This story also gives us some insights into Heaven, Hell, and conversion:

1. Hell is a place of suffering, agony, unfulfilled longings, fire, and regret. Heaven is a place of comfort and community.
2. There are no second chances after this life. Once we die, we go to one place or the other, and there's no crossing over.
3. It isn't *proof* that people need, but *faith*. God's Word doesn't need to be proven, it needs to be believed.

By the way, this is the only story Jesus ever told in which he actually named one of the characters. It's interesting to note that in this story, Lazarus is afflicted with a terrible sickness, dies, and goes to Heaven. In real life, Jesus' friend Lazarus was afflicted with a terrible sickness, died, and went to Heaven (see John 11).

Also in this story, the rich man begs that Lazarus might come back from the dead in order to witness to unbelievers, but he's told that even if this happened, they wouldn't believe. In real life, when Jesus brought Lazarus back from the dead, the Pharisees refused to believe! (In fact, they plotted to kill both Jesus and Lazarus! [See John 12:10.])

Telling This Story to Students Ages 3-7

How Skunk Got Stinky
(a fable to introduce "Lazarus and the Rich Man")

Now, we know that God made skunks just the way they are. But this story tells us what might have happened if God had let them start out smelling pretty instead . . .

Once upon a time, skunks were not stinky like they are today. They smelled beautiful. And they were white and fluffy, not black with streaks of white.

And there was one skunk who was the sweetest smelling skunk of all. His name was Sam the Skunk. He had beautiful white fur, and he was the richest animal in the forest. All the other animals loved to come to his parties where they ate lots of rich, fatty food with Sam the Skunk.

All the other animals that is, except for Thomas the Cat. Nobody cared for him. He was left out of all the fun. And he had fleas. Now, if you've ever had fleas, you know they're not a whole lot of fun at all.

One day, the sparrows came flying in with a warning: "Fire! Fire! A fire is coming! Everyone run far away!"

But Sam the Skunk didn't believe them. "I'm staying right here. I don't believe there's a fire at all!"

Soon, more birds arrived with the same message: "Fire! Fire! A fire is coming! Everyone run far away!"

Well, Thomas the Cat believed them. He ran to the edge of the forest and crawled under the fence to safety. There the farmer found him. The farmer picked him up and carried him to his house. Then he cleaned up Thomas and gave him lots of tuna fish and cool, refreshing milk. He even gave him a flea collar to get rid of those pesky little fleas!

Meanwhile, in the forest, the fire did come! And since Sam hadn't listened to the warning, the fire almost burned his fur! The thick dark smoke covered his white fur so that it looked sooty and black!

Finally, at the last minute, he ran out of the forest to escape, but he was so fat from eating all that rich food that he couldn't fit under the fence!

He squeezed and squeezed until, finally, he made it, just as the fire was coming. And that fence rubbed off the black ashes on his back, leaving a white streak that he still has to this day.

But then, Sam fell into a deep hole where the farmer usually threw his garbage and other stinky stuff.

"Help!" he cried. "Somebody help me!"

Abe the wise old Owl landed by the edge of the hole. "I can't fly in there to help you," he said. "It looks like you're stuck!"

"But can you send Thomas back to warn my brothers about the forest fire?"

"I'm sorry, he's safely in the farmer's house. They can listen to the warnings called out by the birds."

"But what if they don't?" asked Sam.

"Well, then," said Abe the Owl, flying back toward the safety of the barn where he lived, "they'll probably end up in that stinky hole along with you."

And you know what? That's exactly what happened. And skunks have been stinky ever since. And their fur hasn't been white and beautiful anymore either.

And as for Thomas? . . . Well, he's enjoying the farmer's house, his cool milk, and his tuna fish very much, thank you. The end.

After telling or reading the fable, say, **"Now, we know that story was made up. But in the story, why did Sam get into such a bad spot? Right! . . . He didn't believe the birds! Now let's look at a story Jesus told that's a little bit like this fable about Sam and Thomas . . . Jesus' story was about some people who lived very different lives, both on earth and after they left the earth. The name of the story is "'Lazarus and the Rich Man.'"**

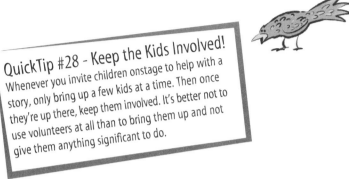

QuickTip #28 - Keep the Kids Involved!
Whenever you invite children onstage to help with a story, only bring up a few kids at a time. Then once they're up there, keep them involved. It's better not to use volunteers at all than to bring them up and not give them anything significant to do.

Here is a sample **story dramatization** of "Lazarus and the Rich Man." As you tell the story, pause and let the children act it out and make the sound effects for the different events within the story.

This story is about two different men.

The first man is rich. Pretend that you're very rich and you're driving around in your cool, expensive car . . . or splashing around in your own private lake . . . or flying your own jet airplane over the mountains . . . Show me how a rich person walks . . . Good! This man lived in style! He had all the best clothes . . . Pretend to put on your rich and expensive clothes! Show them off to the people standing next to you . . .

My, what a fine group of stuck-up rich people you are!

Also, each day at his mansion, he ate as much as he wanted to eat. Shovel some food in your mouth . . . More food! . . . Even more! . . . Wow! You were really hungry . . .

Well, the other person wasn't anything like that. He was poor . . . He had only ripped old clothes to wear . . . Show someone your ripped and tattered clothes . . . Does it make you happy or sad?

He had no home and had to sleep outside. Curl up on the ground like you're gonna sleep on the sidewalk . . . He was also sick and had sores all over his body . . . His only friends were a bunch of dogs . . . Pet one of the little doggies . . . And, of course, the man was very hungry . . .

Well, one day, both of the men died. Lazarus went to Heaven! . . . Show me how happy he was! . . . But the rich man went down below where it was very hot . . . Show me how hot he was . . . He wanted some water. But there was nothing to make him feel good . . . He was sad . . . and he was very thirsty . . . but it was too late for him . . . He hadn't believed in God when he had the chance.

But Lazarus, that poor man, ended up with Jesus in Heaven! He was happy! . . . He had fine clothes . . . lots of good food . . . and best of all, a hug from Jesus! Give someone a hug and tell 'em, "I hope to see you in Heaven!"

Raise your hand if you wanna end up in Heaven with Lazarus! . . . Me too!

OK, everyone sit down and let's talk about Jesus' story . . .

Take a few moments and pray with the children, or share the gospel with them and talk about why Lazarus was let into Heaven.

(Good news! Some of the storytelling ideas for ages 8-12 that appear later in this chapter will also work great with this younger age group!)

		Creative Connection Section
Field Trip Ideas		Lazarus was a homeless man at the start of the story. You could take a trip to a homeless shelter, serve some soup, and then retell this story to everyone there as an evangelistic outreach!
Mood and Atmosphere		In this story, there are two contrasting atmospheres: comfort and suffering—both in this life and in the one to come. Consider having students stand in front of a fan (for Heaven) and then in front of a blow dryer (for Hell) to experience the two different climates!
Sensory Connections	Sight	Show magazine pictures of expensive cars, watches, clothes, or perfume. You may want to videotape a scene from a commercial, home shopping show, or movie that shows rich people leading an affluent lifestyle. (Maybe show pictures of the poor and homeless as well.) Then show the pictures or video clip(s) to your students and talk about TRUE wealth.
	Touch	There are a lot of contrasts in this story between the lives of Lazarus and the rich man. You could contrast rich and cheap clothes by having students feel both silk and burlap and guess which is more expensive. Pull your props out of a dresser drawer—or a suitcase (since we're all on a journey either to Heaven or to Hell)!
	Hearing	Have a few students play rhythm instruments while the story refrains are being said. Consider singing the old spiritual song that's based on this story "Rocka My Soul in the Bosom of Abraham."
	Taste & Smell	To let the students feel the yearning that the rich man felt after he died, you could eat a chocolate bar and drink soda in front of the class as you explain how the rich man longed for the comforts and refreshment Lazarus was enjoying. Watch the mouths of your students water. Ham it up! "These are so good! I wish I had enough for everyone," etc. . . . That unfulfilled longing is how the rich man felt . . . (Or eat fresh, warm, chocolate chip cookies dipped in cool, refreshing milk!)
Costume Ideas		There are a number of characters you could dress like for this story: an angel, Abraham, the rich man, Lazarus, or even a dog! Dress as any of them and retell the story from that character's perspective.

Telling This Story to Students Ages 8-12

One way to emphasize the reversal in this story is to wear a costume that you can actually reverse, such as a vest or jacket.

Or use two contrasting objects—maybe a cane and a plunger! Place a purple pillowcase over the cane (to represent the rich man at the start of the story and Lazarus at the end) and a brown burlap seed sack over the plunger (to represent Lazarus at the start of the story and the other man at the end).

When you tell the story, wave the appropriate object when you talk about the character it represents. Or use it like a director's wand and lead the students in a refrain that the different characters might have said! Then, switch the pillowcase and sack when the story reversal occurs (i.e., when the men die).

Here are two different types of **group refrain** versions of this story.

Happy, Sad, Good, and Bad
(a group refrain/masks version of "Lazarus and the Rich Man")

Notes for the storyteller: You could use the following story script in a number of ways:

1. Present this story as a **masks** story. Every time you say the cue word (happy or sad), everyone pretends to put on a happy mask or a sad mask. (If you have a large group of students, maybe 80 or more, you may wish to split the group in half and have half of the students wear the happy mask, and the other half wear the sad mask.) You might wish to have a partner lead the putting on and taking off of the imaginary masks.

2. Have the students SAY something rather than DO something whenever you say the cue word. Again, the whole audience could say the refrain together, or you could split into two groups. Here are a couple of suggested refrains:

> **QuickTip #29 - Plan Your Pauses!**
> You'll notice that in this story, most of the time when the cue word appears, it's at the end of a sentence. This helps the story flow smoothly and also assists the audience in anticipating their part.
> When you create your own audience participation stories, think through the placement of the cue words so you can make the natural pauses of the story work to your advantage!

HAPPY MASK OR OBJECT
"Alright, baby!"
"Cool!"
(singing) **"Life's been good to me so far!"**
(with huge smiles) **"Now, there's a bright shiny smile!"**

SAD MASK OR OBJECT
"Bummer, man!"
"Boo, hoo, hoo!"
(singing) **"Help! I need somebody! . . . Help!"**
(sadly) **"My life is gloomy and gray!"**

3. If desired, bring two students onstage to be the leaders for each group.

> **Once there were two men. One was rich and <u>happy</u> . . . And one was poor and <u>sad</u> . . .**
> **The rich man had a big house, lots of food, and a comfortable life. He figured he'd always be <u>happy</u> . . .**
> **The other man had no house at all. He didn't have any food, and he didn't have a nice, comfortable life. His only friends were the stray dogs in the city. He thought he'd always be <u>sad</u> . . .**
> **The rich man ate helping after helping of expensive food. That made him <u>happy</u> . . .**
> **Lazarus didn't even get to eat the crumbs that fell from the rich guy's table. That made Lazarus even more hungry . . . and even more <u>sad</u> . . .**
> **Then one day, something unexpected happened . . . both of the men died.** *(lay down the props)*

Angels came and carried Lazarus to Heaven, where he changed. *(switch the props or switch where the two onstage leaders are standing)*

No longer was he lonely or hurting or hungry, or <u>sad</u> . . . . Instead, he was at home, in a palace, at a great feast with other believers from long ago. And he was very <u>happy!</u> . . .

But the rich man was not welcomed into Heaven. Instead, he was sent as far away from Heaven as you can go. And he was no longer rich or satisfied, or comfortable or popular or <u>happy</u> . . .

Instead, he was very <u>sad</u> . . .

So the man who'd been rich was now poor, and the man who'd been poor was now rich! Everything was switched around!

"Oh, please help me!" cried the man who'd been rich. But Abraham, one of the other people in Heaven, said, "I'm sorry, sir. We can't help you anymore. It's too late." And that made the man even more <u>sad</u> . . .

"Then send back Lazarus," begged the man down below, "so that he can warn my family about this terrible place! At least they can end up with him up there, where they can be <u>happy!</u>" . . .

But Abraham shook his head. "They have God's Word in the Bible. If they don't believe that, nothing can help them." That made the man very <u>sad</u> . . .

And so, because of his faith, Lazarus was welcomed home to Heaven. And he lived <u>HAPPILY EVER AFTER</u> . . .

The end.

Listed below is another way to retell this story.

The Day Lazarus Went to Heaven
(a group refrain version of "Lazarus and the Rich Man")

Notes for the storyteller: Invite 4 students onstage. Assign each of them one of the following parts:
- Part #1 - **"I am rich . . ."** *(rub your fingers together as if you have lots of money)* **". . . and you are poor!"** *(turn your pockets inside out)*
- Part #2 - **"I am healthy, . . ."** *(flex your muscles)* **". . . you are sore!"** *(rub your arm as if it hurts)*
- Part #3 - **"I have good things, . . ."** *(two thumbs-up)* **". . . you have bad!"** *(two thumbs-down)*
- Part #4 - **"I am happy, . . ."** *(huge, smiley face)* **". . . you are sad!"** *(sad, frowny face)*

Practice pointing to the children and having them say their parts. You could have the whole group do the parts with the 4 story leaders; or if you have a large group, you could divide the class into 4 groups. As you tell the story, stand behind the leaders and tap them on the shoulder when it's their turn to speak.

Once upon a time, there was a very rich man. He had lots of land and a nice big house, and he was very healthy and successful. And he had a little RHYME [and] he said it all the TIME. It was his favorite thing to SAY, he would say it every DAY . . .

(each time you go through the refrain, cue your leaders and encourage the audience to join along in saying the words and doing the gestures)

> *I am rich and you are poor.*
> *I am healthy, you are sore.*
> *I have good things, you have bad.*
> *I am happy, you are sad.*

Living nearby, there was a poor man named Lazarus who was sick and hurting. He had no food. He had no home. He had no friends. In fact, his only friends were the dogs who would lick the seeping, puss-filled, infected sores that covered his body . . . Hey, it's biblical! Look it up! . . . And when the rich man walked past Lazarus, he would say the little RHYME [that he] repeated all the TIME:

> *I am rich and you are poor.*
> *I am healthy, you are sore.*
> *I have good things, you have bad.*
> *I am happy, you are sad.*

And so, this went on day after day . . . BUT one day, something changed when he said the little RHYME [that he] repeated all the TIME . . .

(notice that this time the refrain changes at the end!)

> *I am rich and you are poor.*
> *I am healthy, you are sore.*
> *I have good things, you have bad.*
> *I am happy, WE BOTH ARE DEAD.*

Because that day, both of them died. And when they died, the angels took Lazarus to his home in Heaven, but the rich man was sent down below, to you-know-where . . .

So then, the tables were turned. Now everything was different for the rich man, because he wasn't rich and happy anymore. But Lazarus was! And now when the rich man saw Lazarus way up ABOVE, in that place of peace and hope and LOVE, he said . . .

> *YOU are rich, and I am poor.*
> *YOU are healthy, I am sore.*
> *YOU have good things, I have bad.*
> *YOU are happy, I am sad.*

After telling this story you may wish to give your students a chance to think about where they would end up if their life stories were to end today (i.e., they died). **"Are you depending on yourself to get into Heaven (like the rich man did)? Or are you trusting in God, through Jesus? Only one way will work. Only one way leads to a happy ending."**

Invite those who have never trusted in Christ to do so.

W.E.G.I. (Weird & Extremely Goofy Ideas)

For an intense way of retelling this story, share it as a **tandem monologue** (two people each share their stories as they alternate speaking parts). Have one person share the story from the rich man's perspective *after* he died and one from his perspective *before* he died, when he thought everything was all peachy keen. Or have the second storyteller share a monologue from the perspective of one of the man's brothers as he lives "the good life" on earth with no idea of what's in store for him in the afterlife.

Typically, when you perform tandem monologues, the storytellers look only at the audience and not at each other. They also freeze while the other storyteller is saying his part.

Perform this at a campfire for your older students. It'll be powerful, moving, and memorable.

Prayer Connection:

1. Pray for those who do not yet believe the truths of Scripture, that they will trust in Christ before it's too late.
2. If you're a believer, thank God that, even though bad things may happen now, he has a great future waiting for you in Heaven!
3. Pray that you would grow in your faith so that you don't doubt God or give up on him during difficult times.

Interactive Prayer Idea:

Share a responsive prayer with your students. Everyone says this line together: **"Lord, help them believe before it's too late."** And then, one at a time, share the names of those you know who are not yet Christians. Between each name, repeat the refrain.

10 The Two Men Who Prayed

BASED ON: Luke 18:9-14

BIG IDEA: Everyone who thinks he's great (exalts himself) will be brought down a few notches (humbled). But everyone who humbles himself before God will be honored and forgiven by God.

GOSPEL CONNECTION: Don't let pride or a judgmental spirit keep you from God. His forgiveness and grace are always available to us, no matter what we've done. Too often our pride separates us from God's love and forgiveness. A repentant heart is a humble heart. Humility is what opens us up to truly receiving God's grace:

> *I tell you that this man, rather than the other, went home justified before God. For everyone who exalts himself will be humbled, and he who humbles himself will be exalted.*   (Luke 18:14)

TOPICS: Confession, forgiveness, humility, hypocrisy, Pharisees, prayer, pride, showing off, sin, stubbornness

MEMORY SPARKS: To find yourself in this story, think of a time when . . .
1. You were distracted in a worship service by noticing how other people were praying or singing . . .
2. You told God about the failings of someone else . . .
3. You were more concerned about maintaining a good image than about expressing genuine humility . . .

To help your students connect with this story, say, "Think of a time when . . ."
1. You refused to admit you did something wrong . . . What happened?
2. You compared yourself to someone else in order to feel good about yourself . . .
3. You looked down on someone because she got caught being bad . . .

HERE'S WHAT'S GOING ON:

Luke places this story immediately after the parable of "The Persistent Widow." Both of these stories teach important aspects of prayer.

Parable	Found In	Audience	Point of the Parable
The Persistent Widow	Luke 18:1-8	Jesus' disciples	We should always pray and never give up.
The Two Men Who Prayed	Luke 18:9-14	People who were confident of their own righteousness.	We should both live and pray with humility. We won't be forgiven until we admit our sins to God.

Don't miss the specific reference to Jesus' intended audience for this story. It'll help you realize which character in the story we're supposed to relate to:

> *To some who were confident of their own righteousness and looked down on everybody else, Jesus told this parable.*   (Luke 18:9)

This is significant. Jesus is not telling this story in order to comfort the afflicted, but to afflict the comfortable. He's not trying to reassure repentant people that God hears and forgives them (although all of that's true, of course!). Instead he's trying to make the proud and haughty aware of their sin.

So here's what that means for you as a storyteller: you need to find a way to retell the story so that your audience identifies with the proud Pharisee. Most of the time when this story is retold, everyone knows from the start that they're not supposed to think like or act like the Pharisee. But that's not the way it was when Jesus told the story. Instead, the people listening were probably nodding their heads and saying, "Yup. I'm glad I'm not like that tax collector too!"

The kicker came when Jesus said, *"I tell you that this man, rather than the other, went home justified before God" (Luke 18:14)*. With that comment Jesus pulled the rug out from under his listeners. *Huh!?* they must have been thinking. *That guy was forgiven!? That sinner was accepted by God!*

That's how you want your audience to respond as well.

HERE'S WHAT THE STORY'S ABOUT:

In Jesus' story, two men (a proud Pharisee and a dishonest tax collector) go to the temple to pray. Both of the men see the same thing—the tax collector's sin. That's good for the tax collector because he confesses and receives forgiveness. But it's bad for the Pharisee because he remains blinded by pride and never notices his own sin.

The secret to retelling this story to contemporary audiences is to find people over whom your students feel superior (just like Jesus did in his story), and then tell the story so that the tables are turned (just like they were in Jesus' tale).

QuickTip #30 - Where Do I Fit In?
In a parable, there's typically one person to whom the listeners are meant to relate. For example, in "The Sower and the Four Soils," we should identify with one of the four types of soil . . . in "The Lost Sons," we'll identify with either the older son or the younger son . . . and in this story, we'll identify with one of the two men who prayed. Usually the context in which the story is told will help you figure out who you're supposed to identify with.

So whenever you're studying a parable, always ask yourself, "Where do I appear in this story? Which character is supposed to be me?" Then make sure your listeners can figure out their place in the story too.

TELLING THIS STORY TO STUDENTS AGES 3-7

To get started, make up a **fable** about a peacock and a sparrow who both go to talk to the fox. One is humble and one is not. Which one draws more attention to herself? What does she do? Which one ends up in Fox's tummy? Have fun creating your own fable! You can do it!

It's often tough to really enter this story and feel its impact because, right away, most of us can figure out who the good guy is and who the bad guy is. However, when we retell this story, we need to remind ourselves that the Pharisee really was a pretty nice guy, and the tax collector really was a crook. But inside their hearts, it was a different story altogether . . .

The Proud Man and the Humble Man
(a storymime of "The Two Men Who Prayed")

Notes for the storyteller: Here are your options: (1) Simply read the rhyming story and don't include any actions, (2) Tell the story and do the actions by yourself, (3) Tell the story and lead the actions with your students, (4) Have a partner lead the actions as you tell the story.

What to say: (read or say with rhythm)	What to do:
Two men went to the temple to pray.	Clasp hands in prayer.
One was a cheater who made people pay	Hold out your hand for some money.
More than they owed him every day!	Weigh money in your hand.
[And] nobody liked him anyway!	Two thumbs-down and shake your head no.
The other man who went to the temple that day	Stand proudly like Superman.
Acted pretty nice and he liked to say	Big smiles. Nod your head.
That he did his best and he tried to obey.	Flex your muscles.
And all the people thought he was pretty OK!	Two thumbs-up.
But when the nice guy went in the temple to pray,	Clasp hands in prayer.
He just talked about himself and began to say,	Point to yourself and look proud.
"Oh, thank you, Lord! Hip, hip, hooray!	Cheer! Congratulate yourself.
'Cause you help me listen to you every day!	Cup hands behind ears and listen.
I'm not like that other guy—glad to say!	Look smug and gesture to the left with your thumb.
I guess I'm the best guy from here to Bombay!"	Two thumbs-up.
But the other man there at the temple that day,	Kneel.
Bent his head low and, without delay,	Lower your head.
Told the Lord he was sorry, that he'd gone astray.	Walk two fingers across one of your palms.
And he asked God for mercy in a great big way.	Hold hands out, palms up.
And Jesus said [that] when they left the temple that day,	Stand and shake your thumb like a hitchhiker.
The second man's wrongs had been washed away.	Wave hands back and forth as if washing.
'Cause the man who was humble had a change of heart,	Point to your heart and nod.
So the man who was humble got a brand new start!	Two thumbs-up and smile!
But the other guy never had a change inside,	Point to your heart and shake your head no.
'Cause the other guy's heart was still full of pride.	Hold your nose high and act stuck-up.
So, whenever you go and decide to pray,	Clasp your hands in prayer.
Make sure that your pride doesn't get in the way.	Shake your finger like a teacher.
Instead, have a humble heart every day,	Point to your heart and nod.
So that all your sins can be washed away!	Wave hands back and forth as if washing.
The end.	Take a bow.

Say, **"In this story, a man showed off by praying aloud about himself. What are some ways kids show off? What are some ways that you show off? What does God think of showing off? What would he like you to do instead?"**

There are lots of contrasts in this story: the posture of the men, the focus of the prayers, the volume of the prayers, the location of the prayers. Here is a **story dramatization** that will show these contrasts to your students. Have half of the class be the proud man and half of the class be the humble man. Pause long enough for the children to act out what you describe. Say,

"When you're proud you're stuck-up. If you're humble, you're not. Let's start by having all the boys act stuck-up . . . Girls, you act humble . . . Now, the proud man walked into the middle of the room—so all you boys come to the middle of the room. The humble man went in the corner . . . Go on, girls, into the corner . . . The proud man pointed to himself . . . the humble man pointed to God . . . the proud man shouted, 'I'm great!' . . . the humble man whispered, 'I'm a sinner' . . . the proud man thought of himself, so you proud people say, 'Me! Me! Me!' . . . and the humble man thought of God, so you humble people say, 'You . . . You . . . You . . .'

"Now, let's switch! If you were proud, be humble. If you were humble, be proud!"
(repeat the activity)

Creative Connection Section		
Field Trip Ideas	A temple, church sanctuary, or other quiet place to pray.	
Mood and Atmosphere	Quiet, reverent, still.	
Sensory Connections	Sight	Sunglasses, magnifying glasses, or telescopes could all serve as good object lessons. • Are you busy looking at other people or yourself? • Where does God look: at the outward appearance or the heart?
	Touch	Pull your props out of a shaving kit (because the Pharisee was very concerned about his appearance).
	Movement	Body positions are important in this story. One man stood tall, the other *"dared not even lift his eyes to heaven" (Luke 18:13,* NLT). Explore these body positions with your students. Examine how they make you feel. How do they relate to Jesus' story?
	Hearing	This would be a good lesson to conclude with music. Play a praise song about the mercy of God, or sing some songs about God's love and forgiveness.
	Smell	Candles or incense burners to create a worshipful atmosphere.

TELLING THIS STORY TO STUDENTS AGES 8-12

To help older students who may have heard this parable before connect with the story on a personal level, start with the following **contemporary retelling** of the story.

Corey's Confession
(a contemporary retelling of the "Two Men Who Prayed")

Important note for the storyteller: This story is retold for middle school (or older) students. It discusses issues that teens and preteens may have to deal with, such as cheating on tests and using drugs. This story is not written for younger children. It will be a powerful story to use with 6th graders, but use your discretion when using it with students who are younger than that.

Creative presentation idea: You could retell this story in your own words (or simply read it as is). If desired, you could use two readers, one on either side of the stage. The different sections of the story are labeled to make it easier for performance by two readers.

READER #1 (preferably a male reader):
Corey Miller glanced over his shoulder to make sure no one was watching. The coast was clear. No one else was in the halls, except for some girl hanging up campaign posters for the upcoming school elections.

He pulled the plastic bag filled with white powder out of his locker and stuffed it into his jacket pocket. *This is the last time I'm doing this. I swear. This is definitely the last time.*

He always tried to be careful when he brought drugs to school. And he was careful who he sold 'em to. But lately, he'd been feeling really guilty. Maybe it was time to stop.

He walked past the girl and nodded.

She just ignored him.

READER #2 (preferably a female reader):

Robyn stood for a moment by the wall, her heart racing, trying to decide what to do. She'd seen the drugs. For a long time she'd suspected Corey Miller of dealing drugs at school, and now she knew.

But what could she do about it? If she turned him in, he and his friends might attack her sometime. They'd been known to do it to other kids who threatened to tell . . .

But if she didn't say anything, wasn't she just as bad as he was? She whispered a little prayer, "Oh, God, what should I do? Should I turn him in?"

Finally, she grabbed her books and headed to the principal's office.

READER #1:

Corey was averaging $500 a week. Sometimes he'd rake in that much in a single day.

He slipped into the rest room and walked over to the third stall. He waited. Finally, the voice came. "Hey, man . . . you got the stuff?"

"Yeah," he answered, "and I'm warning you, don't shoot up and use those pills at the same time. Be easy with it. OK?" Corey had always been careful. Maybe that's why he'd never gotten caught.

"Yeah, whatever."

"I'm serious."

"Some salesman you are. Just hand it over."

He passed the merchandise under the stall and stuffed the envelope of bills into his pocket. But he had a bad feeling about this. Something didn't seem right today.

READER #2:

She paused at the door to the principal's office. Before she went inside, she wanted to make sure she was doing the right thing.

People like Corey were giving her school a bad name. She had to tell someone! They were ruining things for everybody.

Yeah, she was doing the right thing. I mean, she never claimed to be perfect. She made mistakes too. But Robyn had never used drugs. She was proud of how many times she'd said no.

Lots of kids at school smoked pot and cheated on their exams and drank and even tried hooking up with each other. But not Robyn. She and her friends stayed clean. If she'd learned one thing at church, it was how to tell right from wrong.

She grabbed the door handle.

READER #1:

You shouldn't have done it, man! You're a loser! You know that guy is gonna hurt himself! All you think of is yourself! You're getting rich by ruining other people's lives!

Ever since he'd started attending church with his foster parents, Corey had totally been thinking about his life and his choices. He realized that no matter what people thought of him, he needed to make things right with God.

Sweat poured off his forehead. He knew what he had to do. Even before he heard the sirens, he knew.

But when he heard the sirens and saw the paramedics running up to the doors of the school, Corey gulped.

He bolted out of class and down the hall. Behind him he could hear his English teacher yelling threats about how he'd better come back or face another unexcused absence. But he didn't care.

He made it to the rest room just as the police arrived.

READER #2:

Even from the principal's office she could hear the sirens. She slipped back out the doorway and saw the kids gathering at the end of the hall.

READER #1:

Yeah, just as he suspected. Dan was lying on a stretcher. They were giving him oxygen. He'd overdosed.

A group of students stood by watching. One of them pointed at Corey and whispered something to her friend.

In a heartbeat, a thousand things raced through Corey's head. *What a loser you are! You deserve to go to jail. You've been killing people off slowly just to make a few bucks. If this kid dies, it's all your fault! I'm sorry, God! I'm so sorry!* He ran over to one of the paramedics and told him what the drugs were.

"That's a lethal combination!" yelled the paramedic. "How do you know he took that stuff?"

"I sold it to him," said Corey.

"What are you talking about?" the police officer asked.

"I'm the one. I gave him the drugs. Arrest me." And suddenly, he was in tears. A whole lifetime of mistakes had finally caught up to him. "It's not the first time."

Corey hung his head low. But inside, he knew things would be different from then on. The officer just shook his head and led him away.

READER #2:

Robyn saw the whole thing. The cops. The paramedics. Corey Miller being led away. She walked away from the principal's office and just shook her head. *Well, at least he's getting what he deserves. Thank you, God, that I'm not in his shoes!*

She flipped her hair out of her eyes and headed to the lunchtime prayer meeting. Her group was praying for each of the teachers and unsaved kids by name. She could tell them all about Corey and what had happened. Maybe they could pray for him today. He was just the kind of kid who needed lots of prayers.

Just then she noticed a blank stretch of wall near where the crowd of students had gathered at the end of the hall. She pulled out another campaign poster and taped it to the wall: *"Vote Robyn for Class President!"*

She heard one of the paramedics talking about how Dan was gonna be alright. "It's a good thing that kid told us what drugs he used. Or else this guy would have been a goner," he was saying.

Then she glanced at her watch and hurried on her way. After all, she had a meeting to catch and she didn't want to be late.

"I expect to win this election," she thought as she hurried past the kid on the stretcher. "I bet nearly everyone at this school votes for me."

And you know what?

They did.

After all, who wouldn't vote for a girl like that?

After presenting "Corey's Confession," read or retell Jesus' story of "The Two Men Who Prayed" found in Luke 18:9-14. Then ask:

1. Which person in the story could you identify with—Corey or Robyn? Why?
2. Who do each of them represent in Jesus' story? What does that tell you about where you fit in to Jesus' story?
3. What does Jesus' story reveal to you about yourself?
4. What do you need to tell God right now?

If desired, use this quick **fill-in** way to review the story (since many of your students have probably heard it before). Before class, write the following phrases on one side of 7 note cards:

#1 - a cool place to visit

#2 - a cool job

#3 - a job you wouldn't want

#4 - something mean you might do to someone

#5 - something very cruel to do

#6 - something very, very naughty

#7 - a state

Hand out the 7 note cards to your students and have them write whatever their suggestion is on the back of the card (you could do this as they walk into class). Then collect the cards and place them in the correct order.

This is the story of the two men who went to pray . . .

Once upon a time, two men went to the *(flip over card 1 and read whatever it says)* **to pray.**

One of the men worked as a respected *(card 2)*. **The other man worked as a dishonest** *(card 3)*! **The first man said, "Oh, God! I thank you that I'm not like him! I thank you that I don't** *(card 4)* **. . . or** *(card 5)* **. . . or** *(card 6)*! **And I'm glad that I give 10 percent of all I own to people from** *(card 7)*!"

But the other man just stood in the corner and prayed, "God, be merciful to me, a sinner." And that man, and not the other one, went home that day forgiven by God.

The end.

Say something like, **"Following the rules or living a good life isn't what Christianity is all about. It's about humility, faith, and repentance—not image, success, or popularity. None of us is good enough to work our way into Heaven anyway. We're all hopeless until we humbly admit that we need to be forgiven.**

"The first step to receiving God's forgiveness is admitting that you need it. If you have never done that before, will you do it right now?"

W.E.G.I. (Weird & Extremely Goofy Ideas)

Pull out some goofy costumes and have the children dress one person "proudly" and another "humbly." Put mayonnaise and gel in their hair . . . put makeup on them . . . Have fun! Then, discuss humility, appearances, and the condition of our hearts. What does a humble person wear? What does a proud person wear? What makes you say that? How will that change your habits?

PRAYER CONNECTION:

1. Pray for the humility to admit you need God.
2. Pray for the faith to trust in the forgiveness of God.
3. Pray for the courage to say "I'm sorry" both to God and to others.

PRAYER IDEA FOR YOUNGER KIDS:

Today, rather than *saying* your prayers, paint them! Hand out paper and paint (or crayons) and have the students paint a Prayer Picture. Then have them take it home and share their prayer with their family members.

SUGGESTED PRAYER FOR OLDER STUDENTS:

God, I like to think of myself as a pretty good person. But the better I think I am, the less I think I need you. But I DO need you, Jesus. I know I'm a sinner. None of us is good enough on our own; we're all sinners in need of a Savior. Today, God, I want my prayer and my life to echo the prayer of the guy in your story who said, "Have mercy on me, a sinner." Amen.

100 Sharable Parables

The Workers in the Field 11

BASED ON: Matthew 20:1-16

BIG IDEA: We should be thankful for God's generosity to us, rather than resentful and judgmental when he treats others graciously.

GOSPEL CONNECTION: It's only because of God's gracious love that any of us are saved. We're all undeserving. We should be thankful for his love for us, not envious of his love for others.

> *He saved us, not because of righteous things we had done, but because of his mercy. He saved us through the washing of rebirth and renewal by the Holy Spirit.*   *(Titus 3:5)*

TOPICS: Complaining, envy, God's kingdom, grace, Heaven, resentment, rewards

MEMORY SPARKS: To find yourself in this story, think of a time when . . .
1. Life didn't seem fair, but then you realized you were trying to put yourself first . . .
2. Someone else got something you felt you deserved . . .
3. You felt like God owed you for something you did for him . . .

To help your students connect with this story, say, "Think of a time when . . ."
1. You had to work hard to get a treat, but your brother or sister got one without having to do anything . . .
2. You studied hard for a test, but when everyone else did poorly, the teacher curved it so that all your work didn't even pay off . . .
3. You had 10 times as many chores to do at home as your brothers or sisters, but your parents gave you all the same allowance . . .

HERE'S WHAT'S GOING ON:

A rich young man wanted eternal life. He asked Jesus how he could receive it, and Jesus told him to obey the commandments. "I've done that!" said the young man.

Then Jesus told him to sell all he owned, give the money to the poor, and come follow him. When Jesus said that, the young man went away sad, for he had great wealth (see Matthew 19:16-22).

The man's love for a comfortable lifestyle and his spiritual blindness to his own sinful condition were getting in the way of his reception of God's grace. After the man left, Jesus told his disciples that it wasn't possible for a rich man to enter Heaven. Here's how they responded:

> *When the disciples heard this, they were greatly astonished and asked, "Who then can be saved?" Jesus looked at them and said, "With man this is impossible, but with God all things are possible." Peter answered him, "We have left everything to follow you! What then will there be for us?"*   *(Matthew 19:25-27)*

It's true that Peter and the rest of the disciples had given up much to follow Jesus. Some gave up careers (Peter and Andrew), some gave up family relationships (James and John), and still others gave up wealth and prosperity (Matthew). And now, in light of Jesus' words, Peter was wondering, *Will we be rewarded for our sacrifice? What's gonna be in it for us?*

Jesus answered by saying that those who have sacrificed for him in this life will indeed be rewarded: *"But many who are first will be last, and many who are last will be first" (Matthew 19:30).* And then, Jesus told the story of "The Workers in the Field" to further clarify his point.

HERE'S WHAT THE STORY'S ABOUT:

In this story there's a great surprise—a landowner pays everyone the same amount, even though some of them worked much longer than others. Now, we would expect the landowner to reconcile the mistake rather than justify his decision; so when he doesn't, we can easily identify with the grumbling workers who think he's being unfair.

Jesus is telling us to do our work and stop worrying about what's fair or what's in it for us. It's ALL by grace! Yes, we'll be rewarded, but our hearts should be focused on God's grace rather than the size of our reward.

When Jesus says that *"the last will be first, and the first will be last,"* he's saying those who are first now (in this life) will not necessarily be honored in the next. And many who aren't first now (in this world) will be honored in the next. It's a reversal. The things that the world looks up to are not the same things God looks up to.

Remember the rich young ruler who placed his wealth above his relationship with God? Remember the context for Jesus' parable? Well, in this life he may be highly honored and respected because of his wealth, but in the realm of the eternal, he'll lose out because following God wasn't a priority in his life. The first will be last. And the disciples who gave up so much will be rewarded in Heaven. The last will be first.

The people in the story were very concerned about getting their fair share for the work they did, just like Peter was. Remember his comment: *"We have left everything to follow you! What then will there be for us?" (Matthew 19:27).* That's the way the world thinks. But Jesus is saying it's reversed in God's kingdom. We need to stop focusing on ourselves and focus more on God's gracious love. We serve God in response to his grace, not because there's something in it for us. This story is about Heaven, not the rewards we might receive when we get there.

We should be thankful that God has taken notice of us at all. That's what grace is all about. Grace is meant to be received with an attitude of gratitude.

In the story, the landowner gave the men a job because of their need, not his. He gave them a greater purpose to fulfill than standing around doing nothing. That's grace.

Grace is never "fair." That's the point. Grace moves beyond what's fair. God doesn't give us what we deserve (if he did, we'd all be in trouble!). Rather, he's generous and gracious to each of us. Everything we receive from God is *more* than we deserve.

So, in that case, why would we ever complain about the amount of grace God decides to give to anyone else or worry about how much we're getting out of the deal? The irony in all of this is, the more we forget about the reward, the more we'll be rewarded!

QuickTip #31 - Let the Story Speak for Itself.
In your enthusiasm to make sure that your children understand your stories, be careful that you don't over-explain yourself. Very often, the more you explain a story, the less impact it has. In fact, the best stories require no explanation at all because the point of the story is contained within the story itself. There's nothing left to explain.

Of course, that doesn't mean you should leave people totally confused. It just means you can usually let the story speak for itself. Trust the power of the parable to do its work.

TELLING THIS STORY TO STUDENTS AGES 3-7

This story might be tougher for children to understand because they're not used to a work environment. However, they are aware of what seems fair and what doesn't! In fact, you've probably heard kids complain, "That's not fair!" (Usually, they're not as concerned about justice as much as they are with getting as much of the good stuff as everyone else!)

There are a number of concepts in this story that might not be familiar to children:

- vineyard - a place where grapes grow
- a denarius - the amount of money you'd get for working all day
- marketplace - a place where people buy and sell things and look for jobs
- third hour - 9:00 A.M.
- sixth hour - noon
- ninth hour - 3:00 P.M.
- eleventh hour - 5:00 P.M.

You may wish to begin by telling the following **fable.**

The Hardworking Hen

Bawk, bawk, bawk. Henrietta the Hen worked hard. She swept the barnyard. Sometimes she even cleaned out the chicken coop.

Yuck.

And every day, the farmer would give her more food.

But she didn't like it when the other animals like Greg the Duck and Thomas the Cat got just as much food as she did.

"It's not fair," she would complain to the farmer. "I do more work, so I should get more food! I work the hardest, and I've been at the farm the longest! I should get the biggest reward! Bawk, bawk, bawk!"

"But it's my food!" said the farmer. "Can't I give away as much or as little as I like? What right do you have to complain? You didn't end up on the kitchen table, did you?"

"Um, no," said Henrietta. She hadn't thought of that.

"So be thankful! Or next time you might end up joining me for supper!"

And so, from then on, Henrietta didn't complain nearly so much.

The end.

Before telling Jesus' story, try the following **game** with your students. Explain that everyone in the class is going to have a small job. Say, **"I'll give 10 pieces of candy to everyone who works for one whole minute picking up confetti!** (or pencil shavings or crumpled up paper or something else that you scattered across the room before class) **I'll pay everyone who works for 30 seconds, 10 seconds, and 3 seconds a fair amount of candy too. OK! Who wants the 10 pieces?"** . . .

Divide up the class and then begin. Tell each group when to go to work. Finally, when the time is up, line up everyone and start with those who worked the least amount of time. Give them 10 pieces of candy. See how the other children react to that, and then use it as a discussion starter to get them thinking about today's story!

Then, summarize Jesus' parable in your own words. An example is given below.

Once, there was a landowner who wanted to hire some men to work in his fields. It was hard work, and there was a lot of work to be done. So he went into town and found some people who needed a job. They agreed to work for him, and he agreed to pay them.

Later in the day, he went back and hired more people. He did this again and again all throughout the day. He hired them because they needed work.

Finally, he lined everyone up and started handing out the money.

And what do you think happened when he started to give each person THE SAME EXACT AMOUNT?

Right! The ones who had worked the longest complained just like you did!

"It's not fair!" they said. "We worked harder! We worked longer! We should get more money! . . . We worked harder! We worked longer! We should get more money!"

But the rich man reminded them that he wasn't being unfair because he was giving them exactly what he'd promised. They were so busy comparing what they got with what everyone else got that they forgot about his kindness to even hire them in the first place!

Explain that this story is about God's love and kindness to us all. We shouldn't feel angry or jealous when God saves or blesses someone else. Say, **"Those hired first needed to be thankful, not jealous. We can learn from them and from Henrietta the Hen to be thankful to God for all his good gifts to us. And we can remember not to be jealous when God shows his love to someone else."**

A great way to introduce or reinforce Bible stories with young children is by writing parodies of popular children's **songs**. Like this one!

I'VE BEEN WORKING IN THE VINEYARD
(sing to the traditional tune of "I've Been Working on the Railroad")

I've been working in the vineyard,
All the live-long day!
I've been working in the vineyard,
Just to earn a little pay!
Can't you hear the grapes a-squishin'?
[With] juice runnin' through my toes!
Can't you hear the grapes a-squishin'?
Stainin' all my clothes!

Mister, won't you pay,
Mister, won't you pay,
Mister, won't you pay me mo-o-o-re?
Mister, won't you pay,
Mister, won't you pay,
Mister, won't you pay me more?

Someone's gettin' paid some money,
Someone's gettin' paid, I kno-o-o-ow!
Someone's gettin' paid some money.
But I arrived awhile ago . . .

[And I'm] Singin' . . . Fee . . . fi . . . I want more dough!
Fee . . . fi . . . I want more do-o-o-ough.
Fee . . . fi . . . I want more dough.
['Cause] I arrived awhile ago!

	Creative Connection Section	
Field Trip Ideas	Some of the locations mentioned in this story include a marketplace and a farm. Consider retelling this story at a nearby farm, produce stand, or mall. Or tell it at a place where people look for jobs, such as a homeless shelter, a welfare office, or a temporary job agency.	
Mood and Atmosphere	A hot, sunny farm and a busy, noisy marketplace. There is also a contrast in this story between the initiative of the landowner vs. the laziness of the workers, and the kindness of the landowner vs. the grumbling of the workers.	
Sensory Connections	**Sight**	A large bunch of grapes, or some coins, money, wallets, or purses.
	Touch	Let the children hoe a garden, rake leaves from the church lawn, or dig holes to plant some seeds to help them get involved in the story.
	Hearing	Sing or play some work songs (such as the one included in this chapter), or write your own. Or you could sing songs of thanksgiving and praise to God to remind your students to be thankful!
	Taste	Give the children a snack of fruit (strawberries, grapes, or bananas) that might be grown in a vineyard or a farmer's field.
	Smell	Hold up a stinky, sweaty shirt or a pair of old socks. Hold it in a pair of pliers and pass it around so the children can smell it! Say, "That's what hard work smells like! The workers in the story probably wanted more money so they could buy more laundry soap!"
Costume Ideas	Dress up like a rich landowner, a hardworking laborer, or even a giant grape!	
Other Ideas	Have someone who has had a hard time finding a job share with the kids how thankful he was when he was finally hired somewhere. Relate his story to the thanks we should have for God!	

W.E.G.I. (Weird & Extremely Goofy Ideas)

Hand out some funny props (such as duct tape, a jump rope, a pair of keys, and a carrot) and have your students create four frozen scenes from the story. They have to use all the props at some point, and can use people for anything living or nonliving to show you the picture.

Have them choose one scene from the beginning of the story that shows you the main characters, one from the middle that shows you the action, another that shows you the story's struggle (or emotion), and a final picture that shows you the conclusion.

Then, have your students get into position and show you a living slide show of the story![1]

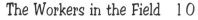

[1] This idea is based on the creative dramatics activity "Frozen Pictures" found in *Act It Out!* by Randy L. Ritz (Standard Publishing, 1999) pages 31–34. If you would like more information on exercises like these, contact Dr. Randy Ritz by e-mailing him at randy.ritz@concordia.ab.ca.

TELLING THIS STORY TO STUDENTS AGES 8-12

Discuss with your students how they'd feel if they worked all year on a big project for school, and then someone else transferred in with a week left and ended up getting the same grade as they did. Say, **"Jesus told a story about something just like that!"** Then transition into retelling Jesus' story.

Or, instead of using a discussion starter to get the children thinking about the issues involved in today's lesson, you may wish to tell the following thought-provoking **folktale** from India.

The Pot of Gold[2]

Once upon a time, there was an old man in India who sat outside his village and stirred a big pot of mud with a long wooden stick. Some people thought he was crazy, and some people thought he was a miracle worker.

Because, the weird thing was, every couple of days he'd reach into the pot and pull out a chunk of gold!

Now, no one knew how he did it. They watched night and day and never saw him put gold into the pot, only pull it out. Finally, a young man asked him how he did it.

"Well, I just put some dirt in the pot, add water, and sit here stirring the mud until the gold appears."

"It can't be that easy," said the young man. "It's impossible!"

"Try it for yourself," replied the old man.

So the young man did just as the older guy had said. He put some dirt in the pot, added some water, and sat there stirring the mud . . . and stirring the mud . . . and stirring the mud. Every few minutes he'd check to see if there was any gold, but none appeared.

"How long does it take?" he asked.

"Well, it varies," said the old man. "Sometimes it takes hours. Other times it takes days."

The young man sat there for a week stirring the mud. But still no gold appeared.

"It's not working!" he complained. "What am I doing wrong?"

"Well, did you do as I said?"

"Yes! Yes," said the young guy. "I did it all! The dirt, the water, the stirring! Everything!"

Suddenly, the old man looked embarrassed and said, "Oh, I forgot one thing. If you want it to work, you can't think about the gold while you stir it."

Be aware that, at first, your students might be a little confused by the ending of this story. Let them think about it for a few seconds; then, if desired, lead a discussion to draw out the truths of the story.

1. What do you think this fable teaches us?
2. How is this story similar to our lives?
3. How could we apply this to our lives?
4. How do you think "thinking about the gold" affects our service and relationship to God? Explain.

[2] This story is based on "A Pot of Gold" from Stories for the Journey by William R. White, Copyright © 1988 Augsburg Publishing House. Used by permission of Augsburg Fortress.

Vroom!

(a call and response/contemporary retelling version of "The Workers in the Field")

Notes for the storyteller: Explain that the audience will have three parts to say when you signal to them (the cue words are underlined):

1. "When I say 'Vroom!' you'll pretend to drive a monster-size pickup truck! (Use hand gestures and engine sounds!) Ready? Vroom!" . . .
2. "When I give you two thumbs-up, you'll say, **'Awesome!'** And then we'll do it a second time, and you gotta do it really loud and wild! Let's try it" . . .
3. "Later in the story when I point to you, you'll say, **'Um . . . yeah!'** in kind of a stupid-sounding voice. Let's practice" . . .

(If you want to include another storyteller, have her lead the actions for the group, or alternate back and forth. You could even adapt the following story into a skit that some of your students could act out as one person narrates the story!)

There was a farmer who wanted to hire some men to work in his vineyard. So early in the morning, he drove his pickup truck to town . . . <u>Vroom</u>! . . . And he said, "Hey, anybody around here want a job?"

And there were a bunch of men standing around doing nothing, and they said, "Si, señor!"

So the farmer said, "Well, hop in!"

And they were like, "<u>Awesome</u>!"

"I'll pay you $100."

"<u>AWESOME</u>!"

So he drove 'em back to the farm . . . <u>Vroom</u>! . . . and they all went to work. Some of the men had to dig up the ground . . . some men had to scatter the seeds . . . and some of the men had to water the garden . . .

About noon, the man hopped in his pickup truck again, and drove back to town . . . <u>Vroom</u>! . . .

There were a bunch more guys there standing around.

"You want some work?"

"Si!"

So the farmer said, "Well, hop in!"

And they were like, "<u>Awesome</u>!"

"I'll pay you lots of money!"

"<u>AWESOME</u>!"

In the middle of the afternoon and at five o'clock he did the same thing. And each time that he went to town, he drove his pickup truck . . . <u>Vroom</u>! . . . he hired the men and they were like, "<u>Awesome</u>!"

And each time he said, "I'll pay you what's fair."

And they were like, "<u>AWESOME</u>!"

So finally, at the end of the day, he had everyone line up—starting with the last guys hired. And, of course, he gave them how much? . . . Right. $100. So the guys who'd been working all day in the hot, hot sun were thinking, *That dude's gonna give us a raise!*

And they were like, "<u>Awesome</u>!"

But as he went along, he gave everyone the same amount—$100.

And they were all, "THAT'S NOT FAIR, DUDE!"

But, he's like, "Wait a minute! It's my money, right?"

"<u>Um . . . yeah</u>!"

"And didn't you agree to work for $100?"

"<u>Um . . . yeah</u>!"

"And can't I be generous if I want to?"

"<u>Um . . . yeah</u>—but it's not fair!"

"You think I should give you more than I agreed to pay you, just because I'm being

kind to them?"

"Um . . . yeah?"

"And you think THAT would be fair?"

"Um . . . yeah!"

And the landowner just shook his head and said, "What, are you a bunch of idiots or something?"

"Um . . . yeah!"

Because you end up LAST when you put yourself FIRST,

But you end up BLESSED when you put yourself LAST.

So if God has saved you, don't be whiny and GRIM,

[But] keep your eyes and your heart focused only on HIM.

Because God's grace is truly <u>awesome</u> . . . I mean, when God saves you it's really <u>AWESOME</u>!

Especially when God finally takes us home to Heaven . . . <u>Vroom</u>! . . .

Good job! Turn to the person next to you and tell 'em "<u>Awesome</u>!"

Another way to present this story would be through a **reader's theatre** presentation. This is a popular technique with preteens since they don't have to rehearse for a long time, memorize lines, or even act a whole lot. They just need to dramatically read their script in front of the group and ham it up a little bit!

Working All Day in the Hot, Hot Sun
(a reader's theatre script of "The Workers in the Field")

Notes for the storytellers: When you lead a reader's theatre story, photocopy enough scripts for each of the readers. You'll need 7–13 readers, depending upon how many students you put in the groups: NARRATOR (girl or boy), PETER (preferably a boy), JESUS (preferably a boy), RANCHER (preferably a boy, you're a rich, kind, Texan cowboy), 1–3 GROUP #1 (preferably boys, you're too-cool, urban rappers), 1–3 GROUP #2 (boys or girls, you're brain-dead idiots), 1–3 GROUP #3 (preferably girls, you're perky, peppy cheerleaders)

Consider having the children wear appropriate costumes. Hand the scripts to the readers and have them go through and circle their speaking parts so they can follow along more easily.

Position the NARRATOR, PETER, and JESUS on the left side of the stage; the RANCHER in the center; and the GROUPS on the right side of the stage. Bring up the stage lights, and then begin when the students are quiet.

TEACHER: **Lights! . . . Camera! . . . Action!**

NARRATOR: **One day, Peter was talking with Jesus.**

PETER: **J-Man?**

JESUS: **Yes, Peter?**

PETER: **We gave up everything to follow you, right?**

JESUS: **Yes.**

PETER: **So, will we be rewarded?**

NARRATOR: **Peter said this because a man with lots of money had been unwilling to follow Jesus. And Jesus had told them that without God's help, it was impossible for the rich to be saved.**

JESUS: **Well, Peter, yes. All those who follow me will be rewarded—**

PETER: **Awesome!**

JESUS: **—The last will be first. The first, last.**

PETER: *(clueless)* **Huh?**

Jesus: Hm . . . Let me tell you a story . . . Once there was a man who owned a lot of land.

Rancher: *(like a cowboy)* I own a lot of land. And I'd like s'more cowpokes out there on the range.

Jesus: So he went to town and met some people standing around doing nothing.

Rancher: Howdy! What are you doin'?

Group #1: *(urban rapper style)* Yo, we ain't doin' nothin'!

Rancher: Hm . . . Would you like a job?

Group #1: *(with rhythm)* Yeah, we need a job!
Yo, we need some DOUGH.
So, we'll work all day
if you pay us BEFO'
. . . we go home.

Jesus: So he took 'em back to his vineyard—

Rancher: Um, ranch—

Jesus: OK, we'll call it a ranch—Took 'em to his ranch—

Rancher: —Thank you—

Jesus: —you're welcome—and set 'em to work.

Group #1: Cool.

Jesus: Well, actually, it was hot.

Group #1: Oh. Hot.

Jesus: Later, he went back again to hire more people.

Rancher: Howdy! What are you doin' there, cowpokes?

Group #2: *(stupidly)* Nothin'.

Rancher: Hm . . . Would you like a job?

Group #2: *(stupidly)* Yeah.

Rancher: Well, come work for me, 'cause I'm glad to PAY! And I'll hire you to work 'til the end of the DAY!

Group #2: *(stupidly)* OK.

Jesus: So he hired those guys too. And he went back again and again.

Rancher: How come you're just standing around here?

Group #3: *(like airhead cheerleaders)* No one has hired us! Hooray!

Rancher: Well, come work for me, 'cause I'm glad to PAY! And I'll hire you to work 'til the end of the DAY!

Group #3: *(cheerily)* Ready? OK! Let's go! . . . Hooray!

Jesus: And so, at quitting time, some men had been working all day . . .

Group #1 *(cool)* Yo.

Jesus: And some had been working for a while . . .

Group #2: *(stupidly)* Hi.

Jesus: And some had only been working for one hour . . .

Group #3: *(excited)* Oh! That's us! Hooray!

Jesus: He lined up everyone.

Rancher: OK, let's pay these cowboys and girls—let's pay these cowpeople!

GROUP #1:	*(rapping)* **Yo, it's time to pay the dough, you know.**	RANCHER:	**But whose money is this, pardners?**
JESUS:	**He had the last ones hired line up first.**	ALL GROUPS:	*(together)* **Yours.**
GROUP #3:	**Ready? OK!** **Let's get the money** **that he OWES** **So we can buy** **more panty HOSE! Hooray!**	RANCHER:	**And don't I have the right to be kind to anyone I want?**
		ALL GROUPS:	*(together)* **No!**
JESUS:	**And he gave 'em as much as he'd promised the others.**	RANCHER:	**What?**
		ALL GROUPS:	*(together)* **OK, yes, you do.**
GROUP #1:	**Yo, cool. He's gonna give us even more!**	JESUS:	**And so, many who are last will be first, but those who put themselves first will end up last.**
GROUP #2:	*(stupidly)* **Yeah.**		
RANCHER:	**And here's the same pay, for you . . . and you . . . and you . . .**	PETER:	**Oh. I see . . . I think . . .**
GROUP #1:	**Hey, wait a minute! That's what you were gonna pay US!**	NARRATOR:	**So, the next time you think you deserve more from God than someone else does, remember—God is gracious to everyone. So think about THAT MORE and YOURSELF LESS.**
RANCHER:	**So?**		
GROUP #1:	**Yo, we worked longer and harder!**	EVERYONE:	*(together)* **The end.**
GROUP #2:	*(stupidly)* **Yeah.**		*(Bow. Fade out the stage lights. Exit.)*

QuickTip #33 - Don't Cover the Lesson!

Many times teachers try to cover the lesson or get through the material. But the real goal should be to get through to your students. And the best way to do that is to work at *uncovering the lesson*. Try to uncover the material your listeners need to learn rather than cover the material someone told you to teach!

PRAYER CONNECTION:

1. Pray for those who have been believers for a long time, that they would remember to be grateful for God's kindness.
2. Pray for those who are new believers, that God would give them confidence and perseverance.
3. Pray for those who are concerned about God's rewards, that they would learn to focus on God's grace rather than on their own efforts.

INTERACTIVE PRAYER IDEA:

Decorate a large poster with pictures or sayings of all the things *about God* that you're thankful for (i.e., his characteristics such as love, grace, peace, etc.). Help the students focus on God as the giver rather than on the gifts he gives.

The Vineyard and the Farmers

12

BASED ON: Mark 12:1-12; Matthew 21:33-46; Luke 20:9-19

BIG IDEA: When the Jews rejected the prophets and even their promised Messiah, the gospel was offered to the Gentiles.

GOSPEL CONNECTION: God has sent his grace throughout the world to all who will receive him. His love isn't just for one group, nation, or race. Each of us needs to accept and receive him personally so that we can enter his kingdom.

> *And they sang a new song: "You are worthy to take the scroll and to open its seals, because you were slain, and with your blood you purchased men for God from every tribe and language and people and nation."*   *(Revelation 5:9)*

TOPICS: Faith, God's kingdom, Israel, materialism, persecution, Pharisees

MEMORY SPARKS: To find yourself in this story, think of a time when . . .
1. You were put in charge of something, and tried to find a way to get it for yourself . . .
2. You didn't listen to God's Word, even though you heard it over and over . . .
3. You took your relationship with God for granted, and then regretted doing so . . .

To help your students connect with this story, say, "Think of a time when . . ."
1. You hurt someone's feelings when he tried to take back his toy . . .
2. Someone took something that was yours and wouldn't give it back . . .
3. You ignored a warning one too many times and finally got in trouble for it . . .

HERE'S WHAT'S GOING ON:

Jesus is nearing the end of his preaching ministry, and his stories are getting more and more confrontational. In fact, when Jesus finished this story, Luke mentions that the chief priests wanted to arrest Jesus immediately *"because they knew he had spoken this parable against them. But they were afraid of the people" (Luke 20:19)*.

The chief priests have set about trying to trap Jesus. They asked him by whose authority he is teaching the people. Jesus could see it was a trap, so he threw the ball back into their court and asked them about John the Baptist's ministry—was it from Heaven or not?

Of course, they didn't want to look bad, so they played stupid. And Jesus, in turn, answered their question by means of the following story. (By the end of the story, you'll see he has answered their question, albeit in a rather roundabout way!)

To explore some of the Old Testament allusions Jesus so skillfully wove into his story, check out Psalm 80:8-15; Isaiah 5:1-7; and Ezekiel 15.

HERE'S WHAT THE STORY'S ABOUT:

In this graphic and shocking story, a landowner (God) repeatedly sends his servants (the prophets) to get fruit from his vineyard (the kingdom). But they're beaten or killed by the tenants (the Jewish religious leaders). Eventually, he decides to send his own son (Jesus), but they kill him too! For all of this, they face judgment upon the landowner's return. As a result, the vineyard (God's kingdom) is offered to others (the Gentiles).

In this amazing story, Jesus does several things. First, he **gives a history lesson**. He summarizes the history of an entire nation and its relationship to God in a few short paragraphs! Rather than share the fruit of God's kingdom with others (as God had intended for Israel to do all along), they tried to keep it for themselves. Then, when God's prophets (i.e., servants) arrived, they treated them brutally and shamefully.

Second, Jesus **predicts the future**. He's obviously the son in the story, and he predicts how the Jewish leaders will treat him: *"So they took him and killed him, and threw him out of the vineyard"* (Mark 12:8).

Finally, Jesus **explains the spread of the gospel** to the Gentiles. The fruit of God's kingdom is not meant to be hoarded, but shared. Israel had been chosen to represent God to the world, not to have an exclusive relationship with him.

Of course, the Jews didn't want any of this to come true. As Jesus closed his story, the people said, *"May this never be!"* (see Luke 20:16).

This story warns us today to respect God's spokespeople and to share the fruit of knowing him. It can also encourage Gentiles as they realize that God's grace and his plan also include them.

Now, it's our job today to spread the fruit around so that many, many people can taste and see that the Lord is good!

QuickTip #34 - Try to Stomach This!

Jesus used food to create powerful connections to his stories and teachings. He often taught at parties, once he turned water into wine, he fed thousands on a few pieces of bread, told stories about vineyard owners, and added spiritual significance to bread and wine at the last supper. Be like Jesus. Look for ways to connect your story to the stomachs of your listeners!

TELLING THIS STORY TO STUDENTS AGES 3-7

To introduce Jesus' parable, you might wish to use this **contemporary retelling**.

There was this guy who built a really cool tree house for the kids in his neighborhood. He's one of those professional wrestler guys from TV, and he did it as, like, a charity thing.

Well, he let a bunch of kids play in there while he volunteered at the local gym. And the kids started acting like it was their tree house! Like they owned it! And when any other kids tried to climb up the rope, they kicked 'em in the face and knocked 'em down.

And when other kids tried to come up through the secret trapdoor, they slammed it on their fingers!

So the guy got really mad. But he was pretty busy, so he sent his son to tell the kids to knock it off. But when the guy's son climbed up to tell 'em, they pushed him out of the tree! He landed on this big rock and broke both of his legs. They had to call an ambulance and everything.

Well, the last I heard, the guy was on his way to the tree house. He was carrying a baseball bat, and he did not look happy.

I know this much: I wouldn't wanna be in the shoes of those kids who tried to take over his tree house and attacked his son . . . That much I know. I can tell you that, right now . . .

QuickTip #35 - Act It Out.

Whenever you find a story that's entirely told in narration without any dialogue (like this one), it's likely that it will be an easy story to act out. Keep an eye out for these types of parables and stories. They'll be popular with your students and easy to adapt into skits!

You could use the following script as a **puppet play,** a **reader's theatre** presentation, or you could act it out as a skit. You'll need 3 storytellers for this drama: OWNER (girl or boy), SERVANT (girl or boy), FARMER (girl or boy).

After photocopying and handing out the scripts, have each reader circle or highlight all of his speaking lines. This will help everyone know when to say their parts. Bring up the stage lights, and then begin when the listeners are quiet.

TEACHER: **Lights! . . . Camera! . . . Action!**

SERVANT: **I just wanted to do what my master told me to do.**

OWNER: **I sent him back to my vineyard to get some fruit.**

SERVANT: **But when I approached the vineyard, the people my master left there to take care of it grabbed me.**

FARMER: **We weren't about to give up the fruit that easily!**

SERVANT: **So they grabbed me.**

FARMER: **We grabbed him.**

SERVANT: **And they started beating me up.**

FARMER: **We started beating him up!**

SERVANT: **Ouch.**

FARMER: **We gave him the old one-two punch!**

SERVANT: **That hurt.**

FARMER: **We bopped him on the head.**

SERVANT: *(rub your head)* **Oh, my achin' brain.**

FARMER: **And then we sent him back to that ol' man empty-handed!**

OWNER: **I couldn't believe what they'd done to my servant!**

SERVANT: **Oh, my achin' brain.**

FARMER: **That'll teach him! It's our vineyard after all!** *(mockingly)* **Na-na-na-na-na!**

OWNER: **It's MY vineyard! And I wanted to share the fruit with everyone. So I sent some more servants.**

FARMER: **We gave 'em all the same treatment.**

SERVANT: **Oh, my achin' brain.**

FARMER: **We even killed some of 'em off!**

SERVANT: **That *really* hurt.**

OWNER: **Finally, I decided to send my own son.**

FARMER: **I guess he thought we'd treat his son differently.**

OWNER: **I guess I thought they'd treat my son differently.**

FARMER: **But we did the same thing to him! And after we beat him up, we took care of him for good!**

SERVANT: **They killed him. They actually killed the vineyard owner's son!**

OWNER: **I'm on my way back to that vineyard now.**

FARMER: **Uh-oh.**

OWNER: **And I'll bet you can guess what I'm gonna do to those farmers!**

FARMER: **Um . . . yikes.**

SERVANT: *(gesturing toward the FARMER)* **Oh, their achin' brains.**

OWNER: **After all, the fruit is meant to be passed around and shared with everyone. It was never meant to be locked up and kept behind closed doors!**

EVERYONE: *(together)* **The end!**

(Smile, bow, and then take your seat.)

When the story is done, you may wish to say something like, **"Kids, Jesus told that story because some of the people tried to keep God's Word and his blessings to themselves. Was that a nice thing to do? No, it wasn't! We need to believe God's story and then share it with others!"**

Creative Connection Section		
Field Trip Ideas	An orchard, vineyard, or farm.	
Mood and Atmosphere	The story happens in a green, growing, alive, vibrant place. But the story is violent, and Jesus' tone is confrontational. This story is meant to shake up the Jewish leaders. And, according to Matthew 21:46, it did!	
Sensory Connections	**Sight**	Go online and print out pictures of grapevines, vineyards, or grapes. Help the children see what a real vineyard looks like.
	Hearing	Make squishing sounds, fight sounds, and the sound of horses clopping. Hand out tape recorders and let your students record their own sound effects for the story; then get back together and have someone narrate the story with the recorded sound effects!
	Taste and Touch	Have a snack of white grape juice, or munch on some grapes when you tell this story. (You could also substitute oranges, lemons, or another juice if grapes aren't available.)
	Smell	Ripe grapes can have a strong, pungent smell. If you buy some grapes and let them sit for a while, you'll have a memorable object lesson for your students!
Costume Ideas	The different characters in this story could each have a different costume: (1) the landowner could wear rich, nice clothes, (2) the farmers in charge of the vineyard could be wearing overalls, (3) the servants could wear simple matching outfits (such as black turtlenecks), (4) the son (if you include him) could be dressed like his father.	
Other Ideas	The servants kept going to the vineyard even though they knew what had happened to the others who went before them. Who do these servants represent from the history of Israel? How should *their* attitude apply to *us* today?	

W.E.G.I. (Weird & Extremely Goofy Ideas)

In Jesus' day, people would make grape juice or wine by squishing the juice out of the grapes by stepping on them with their bare feet! You guessed it! Get some large tubs, some bunches of grapes, and a lot of towels! (Hint - Use this as an object lesson, not as a snack!) It gives a whole new meaning to the word *toe jam*, doesn't it?!

TELLING THIS STORY TO STUDENTS AGES 8-12

Jesus starts his story by saying, *"A man planted a vineyard. He put a wall around it, dug a pit for the winepress and built a watchtower. Then he rented the vineyard to some farmers and went away on a journey" (Mark 12:1)*. Notice all the verbs Jesus used? "Planted . . . put . . . dug . . . built . . . rented . . . went." Because this section is packed with lots of action and only a little dialogue, it's easy for folks to act out as a **narrative pantomime**.

The Greedy Grape Grabbers
(a narrative pantomime of "The Vineyard and the Farmers")

Notes for the storytellers: Before beginning, call up 10–12 volunteers and assign them their parts: RICH MAN (boy), 2–3 FARMERS (boys or girls), 1ST SERVANT (boy or girl), 2ND SERVANT (boy or girl), 3RD SERVANT (boy or girl), 2–3 OTHER SERVANTS (boys or girls), THE SON (boy), WALL (boy or girl).

Position the MAN and the FARMERS on the left side of the stage, the SON and all the SERVANTS on the right side of the stage, and the WALL in the center of the stage.

Sit in the front row of the audience while you read the story. Here's how it might sound with pauses and prompts for the actors:

> **A man planted a vineyard . . . GO AHEAD AND PLANT SOME GRAPE SEEDS . . . LOTS OF SEEDS . . . MORE SEEDS! MORE! . . . GOOD . . . He put a wall around it . . . dug a pit for the winepress . . . DON'T FALL INTO THE PIT! . . . I THINK IT WAS A LITTLE DEEPER . . . and built a watchtower.**
>
> **Then he rented the vineyard to some farmers . . . FARMERS! WHERE ARE YOU? . . . WAIT, DON'T WALK THROUGH THE WALL! USE THE GATE! . . . and went away on a journey . . . GOOD-BYE . . .**
>
> *(based on Mark 12:1)*

As you can see, the comments inserted into the text are responses to what might be happening onstage. You may wish to plan some humorous comments beforehand, but you'll need to watch what's actually happening and be prepared to respond to it. Also, watch your actors so you can give them verbal cues about when to come onstage, exit the stage, etc. . . .

> **At harvest time he sent a servant to the farmers to collect from them some of the fruit of the vineyard . . . But they seized him . . . beat him up . . . REMEMBER, WE ARE ONLY ACTING! NO REAL BEATINGS, PLEASE! . . . and sent him away empty-handed . . . Then he sent another servant to them . . . they struck this man on the head . . . OUCH! THAT'S GOTTA HURT! . . . and treated him shamefully . . .**
>
> **He sent still another . . . and that one they killed . . . He sent many others; some of them they beat, others they killed . . . BY THE END THERE WERE BODIES EVERYWHERE . . . IT LOOKED LIKE THE SET OF A KUNG FU MOVIE . . .**
>
> *(based on Mark 12:2-5)*

Wow. Still no dialogue. See all the verbs? Notice the action? This is the ideal type of story for a narrative pantomime!

By the way, as you probably noticed, this story includes lots of violence. Obviously, you don't want the students to really beat each other up! Although I wouldn't use this story as is with younger children, I would use this story with preteens. They'll probably think it's cool! Just be careful to make sure the story isn't too scary for your students.

> **He had one left to send, a son, whom he loved. He sent him last of all, thinking they would respect him . . . But they grabbed him . . . and killed him . . . and threw him out of the vineyard because they wanted it all for themselves. So what did the owner do? He went and got rid of those tenants . . . So that the fruit could be shared with everyone . . . The end.**
>
> *(based on Mark 12:6-9)*

Instead of (or in addition to) acting out this story as suggested above, you could tell this story as a **group refrain** story. Here's a suggested way to do this in a fun way that involves all of your students.

The Tale of the Evil Farmers
(a group refrain version of "The Vineyard and the Farmers")

Notes for the storyteller: Divide the audience into four groups and assign each group a part. If desired, have them stand up while saying their part. As you teach each part, say it in a silly and exaggerated way. Add actions if you desire. Explain the cue words for each group.

Cue Words: **What to say and do:**
Landowner: *(in a funny vampire-like Transylvania accent)* **"We'll grow some green grapes!"**
Servants: *(sounding really stupid)* **"Duh, would you like some water?"**
Farmers: *(with a crazy, evil laugh)* **"We'll have the vineyard to ourselves! Ha, ha, ha, ha!"**
Vineyard: *(in an itty, bitty grape voice)* **"Oh, no! Don't step on me! Ahh! *(Squish! . . .)*"**

Once upon a time, there was a <u>landowner</u> who planted a <u>vineyard</u>. He put up a wall, dug a pit for the winepress, and built a watchtower.
Then, he went away on a journey and rented it out to some <u>farmers</u>.
At harvest time, he sent a <u>servant</u> back to the <u>farmers</u> to collect some of the fruit of the <u>vineyard</u>.
But they took him, and beat him! And threw him out of the <u>vineyard</u>.
So, the <u>landowner</u> sent another <u>servant</u>. And another <u>servant</u>. And still another <u>servant</u>! Some were beaten, others killed, by those wicked <u>farmers</u>.
Finally, the <u>landowner</u> said, "I'll send my son. Surely those wicked <u>farmers</u> won't hurt him!"
But when the son arrived, they said, "If we kill him, it'll all be ours, forever!" So they took him, and killed him, and threw him out of the <u>vineyard</u>.
And then Jesus told the church leaders, *"Therefore I tell you that the kingdom of God will be taken away from you and given to a people who will produce its fruit"* (Matthew 21:43).
Jesus wants all of us to share the fruit and invite others into his kingdom and taste and see that the Lord is good! Let's all do the grapes' part one more time together! . . . <u>Vineyard</u>!

Take a little time to explain the background of the story and make sure your students can find themselves in the story. Consider having the students create or write a contemporary version of the story. Here's one scenario you might use: There's been an uprising, a revolution. Rebels have taken over an American embassy . . .

"The helicopter hovered for a second above the landing pad and then descended into the gunfire. The embassy lawn was blackened and scarred. One of the mercenaries on the rooftop aimed his machine gun at the helicopter pilot, and pulled the trigger. . . ."

Now, write the rest of the story, trying to retell Jesus' parable in an exciting, contemporary way!
Retelling Jesus' parables can help students remember them, draw out the truths of them, experience them in much the same way the original audiences did, and apply them to their lives.

Prayer Connection:
1. Pray for those who hear God's Word, that it would grow fruit in their lives.
2. Pray for those who spread God's Word, that they would remain faithful to his calling.
3. Pray for Jews who have not yet accepted their Messiah, that they might receive him into their hearts and lives.

Interactive Prayer Idea:
Hand out little containers of raisins and tell the students to share them with their friends or family members as they share the story of the vineyard with them too!

The Ten Bridesmaids

13

BASED ON: Matthew 25:1-13

BIG IDEA: We need to be ready for Christ's return.

GOSPEL
CONNECTION: God gives us many chances to repent, believe, and accept his grace, not because we deserve it, but because of his love and mercy. But the day will come when our second chances will come to an end (either when we die or when Jesus returns, whichever comes first). If we're not ready for him, we won't be able to enter the party:

Man is destined to die once, and after that to face judgment.
(Hebrews 9:27)

Are you ready for Jesus to return? Will you be let into the party or shut outside the door?

TOPICS: Consequences, distractions, faith, God's kingdom, judgment, patience, perseverance, preparedness, priorities

MEMORY
SPARKS: To find yourself in this story, think of a time when . . .
1. At the last minute you realized you weren't prepared for something important . . .
2. You forgot to charge your cell phone and you missed an important call . . .
3. You were caught unaware when something unexpected happened . . .
To help your students connect with this story, say, "Think of a time when . . ."
1. You missed out on a party (or something else fun) because you were too slow getting ready to go . . .
2. You got bored waiting for something exciting to happen . . .
3. You were trying to finish up a big project for school when time ran out on you . . .

HERE'S WHAT'S GOING ON:

Toward the end of Jesus' ministry on earth, his disciples asked him about the signs that would accompany the end of the world. Jesus talked for a while about the signs of the end times, and then he launched into a series of parables (four in all) in Matthew 24 and 25 that all talk about being prepared for the end.

According to Matthew 24:3, Jesus was sitting on the Mount of Olives when he told his disciples this story.

HERE'S WHAT THE STORY'S ABOUT:

In this story, a group of young ladies is looking forward to a wedding reception. Some of the girls are prepared for a long wait, but some forgot to bring extra oil for their lamps. When the party finally begins, only those who are ready are allowed inside. The rest are shut out.

Now, don't get caught reading too much into this story: Were the girls who forgot the oil supposedly believers too? What does the oil represent? What about them *all* falling asleep? What does that signify? And, is all this supposed to be post- or premillennial?

Who knows!

This we do know: the groom represents Christ. The bridesmaids represent us. And the point of this story is simply this: be ready for Christ's return.

Jesus isn't trying to get believers to doubt whether or not they're saved. He made it clear that no one can snatch the elect away from his kingdom (see John 10:28, 29). Rather, Jesus is explaining that many people put off developing a relationship with him, and many of them will run out of time. We should never put off either believing in Christ or obeying him.[1]

It's also significant that the wise bridesmaids can't help the foolish ones get into the party. What's the point of that? Each of us is accountable for our own choices. Faith is personal. You can't get someone else into Heaven by what you believe. Each of us must individually trust in Christ. And we must all remain ready and prepared for the end times to arrive.

As Jesus summarized his story, *"Therefore keep watch, because you do not know the day or the hour" (Matthew 25:13).*

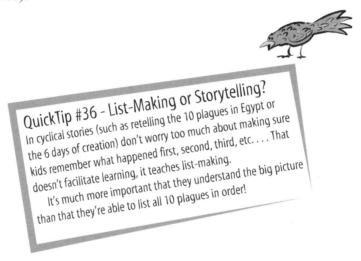

QuickTip #36 - List-Making or Storytelling?
In cyclical stories (such as retelling the 10 plagues in Egypt or the 6 days of creation) don't worry too much about making sure kids remember what happened first, second, third, etc. . . . That doesn't facilitate learning, it teaches list-making.
It's much more important that they understand the big picture than that they're able to list all 10 plagues in order!

TELLING THIS STORY TO STUDENTS AGES 3-7

There's a lot of metaphorical meaning to this story, but for younger children, keep the story simple. Here's the story application in a nutshell: *Ten girls wanted to join a wedding party, but some of them missed out because they weren't ready when the party started. God wants us to be sure we're ready to meet Jesus so that we don't miss out on the party in Heaven.*

Consider retelling this story with simple **props**. Here's a short and easy way of getting at the heart of the story using only 4 common objects!

Getting into the Party!
(a prop-intensive retelling of "The Ten Bridesmaids")

Notes for the storyteller: You'll need a teddy bear, a bottle of bubbles (and bubble blower), a working flashlight, and a watch (or kitchen timer) for this story.

If the comments about lamps and oil don't make sense to your students, talk about flashlights and batteries. You could also involve your students by assigning refrains for them to say whenever you hold up the different items (cue words are underlined):

Teddy Bear - *(smiling and getting all lovey-dovey)* **"Aww!"**
Bubbles - *(to the tune of "Here Comes the Bride!")* **"Dum-dum-da-dum! Dum-dum-da-dum!"**
Flashlight - *(in a big, strong, loud voice)* **"Let there be light!"**
Watch - *(in a tiny little voice)* **"Tick, tock! Tick, tock! Tick, tock!"**

[1] The story of "The Unfaithful Servant" (Matthew 24:45-51 and Luke 12:35-48) teaches a similar lesson to that of "The Ten Bridesmaids." If you're teaching that story, you may be able to adapt some of the memory sparks and discussion ideas found in this chapter and use them with "The Unfaithful Servant."

What to say:	What to do:
One time, Jesus told a story to remind us that we should always be ready for the end of the world to come . . .	Hold up the <u>watch</u>.
Once there were 10 girls who'd been invited to a wedding!	Blow some <u>bubbles</u>.
They knew it would be lots of fun and they couldn't wait!	Hold up the <u>watch</u>.
So that night, they went to wait by the house, just as it got dark.	Hug your <u>teddy bear</u>.
Now, five of the girls had lamps with extra oil so they could burn brightly all night long!	Turn on the <u>flashlight</u>.
But five of them had not brought extra oil. Their lamps would soon go out.	Turn off the <u>flashlight</u>.
The girls all lay down near the house and waited . . . they waited a long time . . .	Hold up the <u>watch</u>.
And pretty soon they got so tired they all fell asleep . . .	Hug your <u>teddy bear</u>.
. . . I'm sure they were dreaming of the party!	Blow some <u>bubbles</u>.
Suddenly, at midnight—	Hold up the <u>watch</u>.
—they heard someone yelling, "The groom is coming! The groom is coming! The party is ready to start!"	Blow some <u>bubbles</u>.
So the girls got up and looked at their lamps . . .	Turn on the <u>flashlight</u>.
. . . but some of the lamps were going out!	Turn off the <u>flashlight</u>.
The girls who hadn't brought extra oil asked their friends if they could borrow some of theirs so they could see their way to the party!	Blow some <u>bubbles</u>.
But the wise girls couldn't give their oil away; they needed to keep their lamps bright!	Turn on the <u>flashlight</u>.
If they gave their oil away, everyone would be in the dark!	Turn off the <u>flashlight</u>.
So the foolish girls went to buy oil as quick as they could! . . .	Hold up the <u>watch</u>.
. . . but while they were gone, the groom arrived and the five wise girls went in to the party!	Blow some <u>bubbles</u>.
Soon the foolish girls returned. But it was too late to get in.	Hold up the <u>watch</u>.
And so, only the girls who were wise . . .	Turn on the <u>flashlight</u>.
. . . and not the girls who were foolish . . .	Turn off the <u>flashlight</u>.
. . . were allowed into the party.	Blow some <u>bubbles</u>.
And Jesus ended his story by saying, "So, stay ready and awake.	Toss your <u>teddy bear</u> behind you!
Because you don't know the day or the hour of my return."	Hold up the <u>watch</u>.
Yes, kids, Jesus is coming back. And, until he does, we need to keep loving him . . .	Go find the <u>teddy bear</u> and hug him.
. . . keep waiting for him . . .	Hold up the <u>watch</u>.
. . . and keep looking forward to the party in Heaven!	Blow some <u>bubbles</u>.
So here is the lesson to live and to LEARN Always be ready for the Lord to RETURN!	Turn off the <u>flashlight</u>.
The end.	Turn off the <u>flashlight</u>.

Listed below is another creative way to retell this story. You may wish to use it as a review after you've told the students the previous story.

The Wedding Party
(a rhyming version of "The Ten Bridesmaids")

Notes for the storyteller: If you wish, act out some of the emotions or movements for the following story. Or, teach the children to say this refrain: ***"Be ready! Oh, be ready for the Lord to return!"*** Have them say it where indicated within the story.

Practice reading this story aloud before class begins so you're comfortable with the rhythm and pace.

(with rhythm)
Ten girls waited for the party to start.
. . . Five were wise . . .
But five weren't so smart.
Now, at first they were happy and excited and glad!
But then they got bored . . .
And tired . . . and sad.

"Be ready! Oh, be ready for the Lord to return!"

'Cause the party didn't start when they thought it would.
(And the girls didn't think
That was very good.)
So all ten girls fell fast asleep . . .
But then . . . at midnight . . .
Comin' down the street . . .

[It was] the party! Oh, the party! It was ready to start!
And the girls got up
To go through the dark.
And the ones who were wise had lamps that burned.
But the ones who were foolish
Started gettin' concerned.
'Cause they just hadn't brought enough oil to burn.

"Be ready! Oh, be ready for the Lord to return!"

No, their lamps weren't bright; they were goin' out.
So they fussed and they fumed,
And began to pout.
"Oh, we need more oil! Give us what you got!"
But the wise girls said,
"We need all that we brought!"

So the five foolish girls all left to get more,
. . . And while they were gone,
The groom closed the door . . .
So that when they returned later on that night,
The five wise ones were all
Locked up tight.

"Be ready! Oh, be ready for the Lord to return!"

"Let us in! Let us in!" said the five outside.
But the door had been locked
By the groom and the bride.
"Go away, you weren't ready," said the groom. "Good night!
'Cause you didn't keep watch,
And your lamps weren't bright."

So . . . the . . . five who were ready all enjoyed the dance.
But the five who were not
Didn't get the chance.
So . . . we . . . need to keep watch, and we need to keep guard.
Through the times that are easy
And the times that are hard.

"Be ready! Oh, be ready for the Lord to return!"

'Cause we don't know the day when the Lord will return.
So here's a little moral,
Here's a lesson to learn:
We need to be ready when the curtains fall,
Or else we won't get
In the party at all.

[Oh,] we need to be ready when the curtains fall,
Or else we won't get
In the party at all.

When the story is done, you may need to explain that the phrase *when the curtains fall* means "when the end comes." Discuss how exciting it is when someone special is coming to visit (like Grandma or Grandpa). Say, **"Do you watch out the window? Do you run out to meet them? Well, we need to be ready and watching for when the most special person of all comes—Jesus!"**

QuickTip #37 - Variety Is the Spice of Teaching!
Avoid using the same storytelling techniques every week. Strive to include a variety of ideas. We all learn in different ways, so spice up your lessons! Use a mixture of drama, games, skits, puppets, props, music, humor, mime, food, costumes, object lessons, and audience participation.
Variety will help cement God's truth into the hearts and minds of your students.

QuickTip #38 - Now . . . Pay Attention!
Always pay attention to the story as you tell it. Don't worry so much about how the story "is supposed to go." Instead, pay attention to how it actually *is* going. Watch it unfold scene by scene.
It's easy to get distracted, but the best storytellers stay tuned-in to what's happening in their stories and continually respond to the audience as they tell their tales.

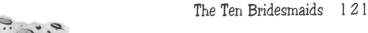

Creative Connection Section		
Field Trip Ideas		Tell the story at midnight at camp. Wake up the children and see how long it takes them to get focused and ready to listen! Explain that when Jesus comes, no one will have extra time to get ready.
Mood and Atmosphere		The emotions in this story go from excited, to bored, to excited, to desperate. Since this story happens at night, you may want to turn off the lights as you tell the story.
Sensory Connections	Sight	A wedding photo album would be a good prop for this story. Talk about how sad someone would be if she were invited, but ran out of gas on the way to the wedding reception (i.e., party) and never made it in!
	Touch	Bring 10 candles (or use flashlights). Light 5 of them. Turn off the classroom lights, hand out the candles, and retell the story as the as the children act it out! If you use a bunch of props, pull them out of a makeup kit or overnight bag!
	Hearing	Sing or teach the old camp song, "Give Me Oil in My Lamp." Write three new verses of your own!
	Taste	Wedding cake! Yummy!
	Smell	Candles, oil lamps, tiki torches, or incense burners will help your students smell the nighttime vigil of the girls!
Costume Ideas		Fun costumes could include a tuxedo, a wedding dress, or pajamas . . . maybe use dunce caps for the foolish girls . . . you could even dress up and give a monologue from the lamp's (or a flashlight's) perspective!

QuickTip #39 - Transformed!
Some story characters are unchanging (we call them static). Other characters are transformed by the events of the story (we call those characters dynamic). To figure out who the main character of a story is, look for the person(s) who is (are) transformed by the events of the story (or *will* be transformed in the aftermath of the story).

Almost always, the main character of a story is dynamic, and the secondary characters are static.

TELLING THIS STORY TO STUDENTS AGES 8-12

This parable is pretty blunt: those who aren't ready for Christ's return are gonna regret it. Consider making up a modern story about some people in North Carolina who know that, sometime during the night, a hurricane is gonna hit the coast. How do the two different groups prepare? What happens to the ones who don't get ready? Act it out dramatically. Include real buckets of water, fans, and flying objects (soft ones) for the storm!

The 10 young girls in this story were probably junior high age girls. To get a good picture of what's happening in this story, picture a bunch of 8th graders at a sleepover! This next story might help you do just that!

W.E.G.I. (Weird & Extremely Goofy Ideas)

Make up a skit about girls getting ready for prom night. Some of them remember to charge their cell phones, and some don't. When their dates try to call, only a few of them get the message. Have teen volunteers act it out!

Or rewrite the story with 10 guys instead of 10 girls. The coach is on his way to the gym. All the guys are in a weight room . . . and what are they doing? Well, they're waiting (what else would you do in a *weight* room) . . .

The Night of the Sleepover
(a narrative pantomime of "The Ten Bridesmaids")

Notes for the storytellers: Invite 7–11 volunteers onstage and assign them their parts. It'll be lots of fun to have some of the foolish girls be played by guys with wigs!

Cast: 1–2 WISE BRIDESMAIDS (girls or boys, preferably adults), 1–2 BRIGHT LAMPS (girls or boys, preferably kids), 1–2 FOOLISH BRIDESMAIDS (girls or boys, preferably adults), 1–2 DIM LAMPS (girls or boys, preferably kids), 2 DOOR (girls or boys), 1 GROOM (boy).

This would be a great skit for your teenage helpers to lead. Or, you might want to do it on a family night and invite some parents to be the volunteers!

Assign each of the WISE BRIDESMAIDS a BRIGHT LAMP, and each of the FOOLISH BRIDESMAIDS a DIM LAMP.

Explain that whenever you say "burning bright," the BRIGHT LAMPS will say, **"Give me oil in my lamp, keep me burnin'."** But when you say "pretty dim," the DIM LAMPS will say, **"Duh, we're rather dim."** (You could also have the BRIDESMAIDS say, on cue, "Whatever!" or "I am so sure!" or "As if!" or another popular teenage saying in your region of the country.)

Start the skit with the DOOR onstage facing the audience at a 45-degree angle (so that when the foolish girls try to open it, the audience can watch). The DOOR consists of two people standing shoulder to shoulder. Instruct one of them to form a keyhole by holding her thumb and forefinger in a circle. The GROOM begins offstage, everyone else is on center stage.

If desired, use makeup, lipstick, panty hose, and quarts of motor oil (for the BRIGHT LAMPS) as props.

Then, read or tell this story . . .

One night, a bunch of bridesmaids *(or say "teenage girls")* **were lounging around waiting outside the doorway for a wedding to start . . . They were putting on lipstick . . . and poofing their hair . . . and pulling on their panty hose!** . . . *(have them pull on the nylons over their clothes!)* . . . **Sometimes they even put makeup on each other!** . . .

Now, half of the girls had brought extra oil for their lamps . . . Hold up your oil! . . . **Their lamps were** <u>burning bright</u> . . . **And half of the girls didn't bring extra oil, and their lamps were** <u>pretty dim</u> . . .

Well, the groom took a long time getting there, and all the girls yawned . . . lay down . . . and went to sleep . . .

They snored really loudly . . .

At midnight, a man yelled for them to wake up . . . WAKE UP! and they all stood up . . . picked up their lamps . . .

And the wise girls' lamps were <u>burning bright</u> . . . **but the dumb girls' lamps were** <u>pretty dim</u> . . .

So the stupid girls asked the other girls for oil, but they refused. They needed oil for their own cars—I mean—lamps.

Finally, the foolish girls left to buy more oil . . . carrying their lamps . . .

That's when the groom arrived! He opened the door . . . led the five wise girls into the party! . . . **The girls carried their lamps through the doorway . . . And then, the groom shut the door . . . And they dropped their lamps . . .**

Soon the foolish girls returned, carrying their lamps . . . which were <u>pretty dim</u> **alright . . .**

They tried to open the door, but it wouldn't move . . . They tried crawling under the door . . . they even tried climbing through the keyhole! . . . **All the while carrying their lamps . . .**

But none of that worked. So they banged on the door . . .

When they begged to come in, the groom shook his head . . . The wise girls shook their heads . . . The bright lamps shook their oil . . .

And so, the foolish girls and their lamps were locked out. They cried like a bunch of babies . . .

But inside, the wise girls and the groom danced up a storm! . . .

The end.

When you're done, be sure to emphasize the point of the story. Say, **"When you least expect him, expect him. Keep watch for Jesus to return! And be ready!"**

Tales of the Smart and the Stupid
(a human clay retelling of "The Ten Bridesmaids")

For a fun follow-up activity with your students, try this **human clay** storytelling idea! Invite 4–6 volunteers onstage. Match boys up with boys and girls with girls. (You could have everyone in the class participate, but it's so much fun to watch that you'll probably just want a few volunteers onstage so everyone else can enjoy the show!)

Say, **"OK, whichever of the two of you has worse-smelling breath gets to be the potter, and the other person gets to be the clay! As I tell the story, you'll see that the characters move through lots of different emotions.**

"As the character in the story feels certain emotions, I want you to shape your clay into the same emotion! Be gentle shaping them and don't just shape their faces, but their whole bodies! Each time when you're done shaping your clay, step back out of the way so the audience can see your sculpture. OK, let's get started!"

Once there were 10 girls who were all looking forward to going to a wedding reception! They couldn't wait to go! They were <u>so excited they almost wet their pants</u>! . . . (Go on, make your clay look excited!)

Now back then, the groom would lead a dance down the streets to let everyone know when the party was gonna begin. And all those girls wanted to <u>dance, dance, dance</u>! . . . (Go ahead! Strike your favorite dance pose!)

But the groom was a long time coming. And the longer it took, <u>the more bored they got</u>.

Soon, all 10 of them fell <u>asleep</u> . . . (Keep your clay standing up though, so we can see 'em . . .)

At midnight, they heard someone yelling for them to wake up because the groom was coming! The party was about to begin! They woke up and were <u>excited</u> again! . . . They all thought of how much fun they'd have <u>dancing</u>!

They grabbed their lamps and set off to join the fun. Now, five of the girls had remembered to bring extra oil for their lamps. They were <u>smart . . . and they were happy</u>.

But five of the girls hadn't planned on such a long wait. Their lamps were going out. They were pretty <u>stupid</u>.

"Let us have some oil for our lamps!" they cried. They were <u>desperate</u> . . . (let's see you look desperate . . . Good . . .) and they pleaded with the smart girls!

But the smart girls said, "We need ours. Go buy your own!" So the stupid girls did. But when they left they were all <u>angry</u> . . .

While they were gone, the groom arrived and the party began! All the smart girls were <u>excited</u>! . . . And began to do their favorite <u>dance</u> . . . just like they'd been hoping for!

Later on, the stupid girls arrived and tried to get into the party, but the doors were already locked. They were <u>so sad they started to cry</u> . . .

(OK, potters, step back for a second . . .)

Oh, the doors had been closed and the party'd BEGUN,
So the ones who weren't ready couldn't join [in] the FUN.
"So keep watch," said the Lord, "every day you're ALIVE,
For you don't know the hour when the end will ARRIVE."

OK, potters, make your clay <u>look watchful</u> . . .
Good job, everyone! Give the potters and the clay a big hand! . . .

When you're done with the story, discuss what it means to be watchful and ready for Jesus. What could we do to help us be more ready? What are some of the things that we do that show *we're not* being watchful? What will you do about that?

Prayer Connection:

1. Pray for those who are not yet ready for Christ's return.
2. Pray for the grace to keep watch and live each day as if it might be your last.
3. Pray for the patience and perseverance to stick with God, even when he seems slow in coming or in answering your prayers.

Interactive Prayer Idea:

Light a candle and pray by candlelight. Pray that God will help you let your light shine until the day he returns to this dark world.

The Ten Bridesmaids 125

14 The Servants and the Bags of Gold

BASED ON: Matthew 25:14-30 (and Luke 19:11-27)[1]

BIG IDEA: We should work hard and be faithful in serving God by using the gifts and opportunities he has given to us.

GOSPEL CONNECTION: In this story, the timid man was the one who was chastised. Those who are afraid to give God their lives, their trust, and their futures will one day regret it. Instead, each of us who believes in Christ must learn to live for him and work to expand his kingdom even when it doesn't seem sensible or practical:

Each one should use whatever gift he has received to serve others, faithfully administering God's grace in its various forms. (1 Peter 4:10)

TOPICS: Consequences, faithfulness, fear, giftedness, God's kingdom, priorities, responsibilities, rewards, risk-taking

MEMORY SPARKS: To find yourself in this story, think of a time when . . .
1. You were put in charge of something, and you didn't take care of it like you should have . . .
2. Someone gave you an important job, but you were too lazy to do it right . . .
3. You put off serving God in some specific way because it seemed too risky, impractical, or inconvenient . . .

To help your students connect with this story, say, "Think of a time when . . ."
1. You got in trouble because you didn't do something you were supposed to do . . .
2. You decided to play it safe, and you later regretted it . . .
3. You were afraid to serve God, so you didn't . . . What happened? How did you feel?

HERE'S WHAT'S GOING ON:

This story occurs in Jesus' explanation of the signs of the end times and is a complementary story to "The Ten Bridesmaids" (Matthew 25:1-13). In that parable, Jesus emphasized how important it is *to be alert* as we await Christ's return. In this story, Jesus emphasizes how important it is *to be active* while we await his return. We need to faithfully use the gifts and resources God has given us to help his kingdom grow.

The audience, once again, is the disciples.

HERE'S WHAT THE STORY'S ABOUT:

A rich man leaves three of his servants in charge of different amounts of his money while he's gone. Two men trade and invest the money, bringing handsome returns. One, however, buries the money and returns it without interest to the landowner. In the end, he's punished severely for playing it safe (Jesus calls him wicked, lazy, and worthless!). The others are commended for putting their money to work.

What's the point of this story for us? Well, first of all, those who are lazy in using the gifts God has given them will regret it. Secondly, service toward God requires courage, faith, and vulnerability.

---

[1] Luke records a slightly different version of this story than Matthew does. This chapter is based primarily on Matthew's account.

Thirdly, if we don't use our gifts, we'll lose 'em because whatever we hold back from God will eventually be held back from us! And finally, never put off serving God until an opportune time. Always serve him now, never later.

Some Bible translations refer to the bags of gold as "talents." This term might be confusing to your students. In Jesus' parable, the word *talent* refers to an amount of money, not a specific ability. Rather than using the word *talent*, just say "bags of gold" (as the *New Living Translation* does). It'll be much easier for your students to understand.

Whatever resources God has given you—time, money, abilities, spiritual gifts—should be invested in serving him. As Jesus pointed out on a different occasion, *"From everyone who has been given much, much will be demanded; and from the one who has been entrusted with much, much more will be asked" (Luke 12:48).*

People bury their talents in lots of different ways: putting off serving God . . . doing what's practical and sensible by the world's standards rather than what's meaningful by God's standards . . . staying in a job you don't feel called to do just to make ends meet, when God has gifted you to serve him elsewhere . . .

> *Whatever you do, work at it with all your heart, as working for the Lord, not for men.*
> *(Colossians 3:23)*

Help your students see how they might be burying the gifts God has given them. And then, help them bring their talents to the surface and share them with other people to help God's kingdom grow!

QuickTip #40 - Tell the Stories That Matter to You.
Every story that you tell should matter to you. Not every story will grab your attention for the same reason, but each story needs to be significant to you. If you don't care about the story, no one else will. Whether you love it or hate it, you need to be emotionally connected to it.

Tell the stories that move you. They may fill you with joy and thanksgiving, or even dread and alarm. Whatever it is, let the story connect with you on a personal level. If you don't, you'll have a hard time sharing the story in a way that will move your listeners.

TELLING THIS STORY TO STUDENTS AGES 3-7

Say, **"Today's story is about a man who let someone else use some of his money. And one of the men was afraid of what would happen if he lost it . . . Let's find out what happens in Jesus' story of 'The Servants and the Bags of Gold.'"**

The Bags of Gold
(a reader's theatre version of "The Servants and the Bags of Gold")

Notes for the storytellers: You'll need 4 people to read this script: RICH MAN (preferably a boy), 1ST SERVANT (girl or boy), 2ND SERVANT (girl or boy), 3RD SERVANT (girl or boy).

After photocopying and handing out the scripts, have each reader circle or highlight all of his speaking lines. This will help everyone know when to say their parts. Bring up the stage lights, and then begin when the listeners are quiet.

TEACHER: Lights! . . . Camera! . . . Action!

RICH MAN: I was going on a trip, so I left my money with three of my workers.

1ST SERVANT: He gave me five bags of gold!

2ND SERVANT: He gave me two bags!

3RD SERVANT: He only gave me one.

RICH MAN: I gave 'em each what they could handle—

3RD SERVANT: Gee, thanks.

RICH MAN: —then, I left for vacation.

1ST SERVANT: I went to town right away and used the money wisely. And I earned five more bags of gold for my boss!

2ND SERVANT: I went to town too. I bought and sold things and earned two more bags of gold for my boss.

3RD SERVANT: Me? I was scared. I buried the gold in a hole in the ground so I wouldn't lose it. Hee, hee, hee, hee . . . Pretty smart, huh?

RICH MAN: Then, when I got back from my trip—

1ST SERVANT: —He was gone a long time—

2ND SERVANT: —No kidding—

3RD SERVANT: —I thought he'd never get back!—

RICH MAN: —When I got back from my trip, I called in my workers and said, "What did you do with the money I loaned you?"

1ST SERVANT: You gave me five bags of gold, and I earned five more!

RICH MAN: Great! You did good with a little, so I'll give you some MORE! You're gonna be richer than ever BEFORE!

2ND SERVANT: Then he turned to me . . .

RICH MAN: . . . And how well did you do?

2ND SERVANT: You gave me two bags of gold, and I earned two more!

RICH MAN: Great! You did good with a little, so I'll give you some MORE! You're gonna be richer than ever BEFORE!

3RD SERVANT: Then he asked me how I did . . .

RICH MAN: . . . And how much did you earn?

3RD SERVANT: Well, I was scared I'd lose it . . .

RICH MAN: . . . And?

3RD SERVANT: And I knew you were a hard worker and you wouldn't like that . . .

RICH MAN: . . . And?

3RD SERVANT: . . . And so . . . just to be safe . . . I . . . um . . . well, I buried it in the backyard.

RICH MAN: What?!

3RD SERVANT: I buried it in the backyard.

RICH MAN: Why didn't you at least put it in the bank so I could've gotten a little extra money?!

3RD SERVANT: Um, well—

RICH MAN: You're a bad worker!

3RD SERVANT: I am?

RICH MAN: And a lazy one too!

3RD SERVANT: Oops. Maybe I'll do better next time.

RICH MAN: There isn't gonna be a next time!

1ST SERVANT: Then he gave me that guy's bag of gold!

3RD SERVANT: I wish there was a next time.

RICH MAN: Do good with a little and you'll get even MORE! So that you'll have more gifts than ever BEFORE! But those who are lazy and don't do their PART, Will lose what little they had at the START!

2ND SERVANT: Then, he threw that guy outside of the house.

3RD SERVANT: Um, it's rather dark out here.

1ST SERVANT: Where no one is happy and everyone is sad.

3RD SERVANT: Um, I'm scared of the dark . . .

RICH MAN: The end.

3RD SERVANT: Hey, wait a minute! Don't I get a second chance or anything?

RICH MAN: Nope.

3RD SERVANT: I gotta stay here in the dark?!

RICH MAN: Yup.

3RD SERVANT: But that's not a very good place to end the story! It's not a very happy ending!

1ST & 2ND SERVANTS: *(together)* It is for us!

3RD SERVANT: But it's not for me!

RICH MAN: Well, that's the way it will be for all those who are lazy with the gifts God gives to them.

3RD SERVANT: I really wish there was gonna be a next time . . .

RICH MAN: Do good with a little and you'll get even MORE!

1ST SERVANT: So that you'll have more gifts than ever BEFORE!

2ND SERVANT: But those who are lazy and don't do their PART,

3RD SERVANT: Will lose what little they had at the START!

EVERYONE: *(together)* **The end.**

(Bow. Fade out the stage lights. Exit.)

To review the story, act it out by doing a **story dramatization** with the students. Act out what it's like to carry all that gold . . . to travel to town . . . to carry even more gold back to the master's house . . . (or to bury that gold in the field . . .) and then to wait a long time . . . and finally to greet the master after his long journey . . . and to hear the good news . . . (or the bad news . . .).

This would also be a good story to tell as a **monologue**. You could choose to do the monologue from the perspective of one of the four main characters, or as a squirrel who uncovers the buried gold when he's trying to bury his nuts!

Or you could tell the story from the point of view of the bag of gold that was buried: "At first I was really excited! I mean, when the master started handing out money, I thought, *This is my big chance! There will finally be some* change *in my life!* But then . . ."

	Creative Connection Section	
Field Trip Ideas	Take a trip down the hallway or to another part of the building. Then talk about the long trip the master in this story took. Discuss who in the story is like Jesus . . . and who is like us . . . Ask, **"Which servant will you be like when the master returns?"**	
Mood and Atmosphere	Celebration for the faithful servants and sadness for the unfaithful one.	
Sensory Connections	**Sight**	If you have a "change bag" for doing magic tricks, use it to tell this story. Change 5 coins into 10, 2 into 4; and then at the end, make the 1 coin of the last servant disappear forever!
	Touch	Hold up or pass around any items that you might use for digging (shovels, hoes, etc.). If you have sandboxes on your property, consider burying small objects that relate to the story. Then have a treasure hunt! A metal detector would also make a great prop for this story!
	Hearing	The jingle of gold, coins, or of a cash register.
	Taste	Buy a package of foiled-wrapped chocolate coins. Have them as a snack as you talk about serving God and not wasting the time and gifts he's given us!
	Smell	Bring a charred and burned log as an object lesson for "The White Fire" story (see the next section), or tell the story around a campfire.
Costume Ideas	Since the man buried his treasure, you could build your whole lesson around buried treasures. Dress up like a pirate with an eye patch and everything! Or dress up like you're ready for a day at the beach.	
Other Ideas	Use a beach umbrella, suntan lotion, a beach chair, and a cooler. Talk about losing things in the sand, and then tell the story of how the unfaithful servant buried his gold and ended up losing it. . . .	

TELLING THIS STORY TO STUDENTS AGES 8-12

Before class, photocopy and cut out enough Story Cards on page 132 for your class.

To introduce Jesus' parable of "The Servants and the Bags of Gold," read or tell the following **fable.** Make it into a game. Say, **"When I read this story, see if you can guess which of Jesus' stories it's like . . ."**

The White Fire[2]

Three men stood before the Angel of the Lord and asked for the gift of his white fire.

"Take it and keep it and use it!" said the Angel of the Lord.

"We will! We will!" shouted the men. And they went on their way.

Each man walked the path before him, and the first man came to a dark and lonely valley. In the valley were many other men, all seeking their way. But with no light, they were hopeless and cried, "If only we had light to show us where to go!"

And the first man said, "I have a light I can share."

And he took the fire that was given to him by the Angel of the Lord, and he made a torch. He held it above his head, and it flashed through the darkness like a sword. And he showed them the way, leading them through the night to the dawn of a brand-new day.

The second man walked another path of the way, and it led him over a bleak moor where the wind blew bitter and cruel and bit at your skin with a thousand teeth. And here there were children shivering in the cold, huddling together for warmth, yet finding none. For they had no fire. And they cried out together, "Without any fire we'll die!"

So the second man said, "I have a fire I can share."

And he took the fire that had been given to him and laid it out before them. He piled up sticks and brush and logs and made a roaring fire that blazed high and bright. And the children gathered around it and held out their hands and forgot the bitter wind.

The third man walked another path of the way. And he said to himself, "How shall I keep my fire safe, that no fierce wind can blow it out? I know what I'll do. I'll hide it in my heart, so that no harm can come to it."

So he hid the fire in his heart and walked along the way.

At last the three men came to the end of the way, and before them stood a figure veiled in white. And he asked the first man, "Where is your fire?"

The man said, "I found some men lost in the darkness, and I made a torch of my fire. I showed them the way. And I thought that my fire was used up, but still it continues to burn."

"Yes," said the one in white, "now it shall never die."

Then he turned to the second man. "Where is your fire?"

"I found children shivering in the cold," he said. "They had nothing to warm them, so I gave them my fire, yet still it continues to burn."

"Good," said the one in white. "Your fire shall never die."

Then the third man stepped forward and said boldly, "I've brought my fire safely through my journey! Through trouble and danger, through peril and strife! And here it is, in my heart!"

Then the one in white pulled off the veil, and it was the Angel of the Lord himself. "Oh no!" he said. "What is this you have done?"

And he opened the man's heart. And inside, it was black and charred, with white ashes lying in it.

After telling the story of "The White Fire," ask the students what they think the story means. Explain that Jesus often used stories to warn people about the consequences of their choices and lifestyles, just like this fable does. Then ask them if they can think of any Bible stories that teach the same truths brought out in this old fable.

[2] Based on "The White Fire 1" by Laura E. Richards, from *The Silver Crown: Another Book of Fables* (Little Brown and Company, 1906), pages 90–93. This book and story are in the public domain.

Then divide the students into groups of 4 or 5 people. Give each group one of the Story Cards below. (By the way, you could use these Story Cards with nearly any story that you're studying, so keep them on hand for other lessons in the future!)

Story Cards
(an interactive, add-on storytelling activity)

Notes for the teacher: Tell the students to read Matthew 25:14-30. Explain that Jesus is telling this story to his disciples to explain what things will be like at the end of time.

Say, **"You have 10 minutes to prepare your story! Ready, go!"** (Depending on the reading ability of your students, you may wish to read the story aloud as a class, before setting a time limit.)

As they're working on their projects, go from group to group, encouraging them or giving ideas if they can't seem to think of anything to do.

Story Card #1 - Act It Out!
Choose one person from your group to be the narrator. As he or she tells the story, have the other people act it out. Tell the story in your own words. In your story use 5 unusual props that you can find in this room!

Story Card #2 - Frozen Poses!
Create 3 frozen scenes from this story. In each scene, you must use everyone in your group. Try to show the most exciting or emotional scenes from the story. Be ready to hold each scene frozen for 10 seconds.

Story Card #3 - Singer/Songwriter!
Rewrite this story to the tune of a famous kids' song such as "Row, Row, Row Your Boat," "Jingle Bells," or "Yankee Doodle." Come up with your own goofy actions, and then get ready to sing the song together to the rest of the class!

Story Card #4 - Add-on Storytelling!
Take turns telling the story. Each person says only one line or sentence of the story. It can be fun if you give one or two people in your group a simple word to say such as "Cool!" or "Bummer!" Try to retell the story so that whenever it gets to either of them, it actually makes sense to say their word!

Story Card #5 - Sound Effects!
Have two people tell the story, taking turns speaking. Everyone else in your group does sound effects and cheers or boos at the appropriate times.

After the students have developed their ideas, gather together as a large group and let each group perform for the rest of the class (or for another class!). By the end of your lesson, the students will have studied this story in depth and reviewed it at least five times without even realizing it!

QuickTip #41 - Preparation!
When you don't spend enough time preparing your story, you may forget key sections, pause too frequently or in the wrong places, repeat words, string sentences along with the word *and* (I've heard entire stories that are all one sentence!), or switch the voice or posture of different characters.

You can eliminate most of these common mistakes simply by practicing your story a few extra times before performing it.

W.E.G.I. (Weird & Extremely Goofy Ideas)

Since the third man in this story buried his treasure, you may wish to play one of the following buried treasure messy games!

(1) **Flour Power** - Bury M & Ms® chocolate candies in two large bowls of flour. Then have two students come forward and try to get the candy out by blowing the flour away. (Or try gum balls buried in powdered sugar. Or sliced pickles covered in mustard.) The students can't use their hands!

(Be prepared for a lot of flying flour!)

(2) **Bear-ied Treasure** – Bury gummi bears in big bowls of chocolate pudding. The first person to find 10 of them wins! Again, no hands! (Have towels available to clean off chocolate faces!)

PRAYER CONNECTION:

1. Pray for the courage to use your gifts for God, even when it seems scary.
2. Pray for forgiveness for all the times you haven't been faithful in serving Jesus.
3. Pray for the faith to serve God even when it doesn't seem to make sense.

INTERACTIVE PRAYER IDEA:

Give all of the students a penny as a reminder of today's story. Tell them that God asks us to serve him and that he'll be more than fair in rewarding all believers. Show them where it says "In God We Trust" on the penny, and let that be their motto for the week!

15   The Sheep and the Goats

BASED ON: Matthew 25:31-46

BIG IDEA: When we show acts of compassion to others, we're actually serving Christ himself.

**GOSPEL
CONNECTION:**   Living lives of love should be the way of life for all genuine believers. Whenever we serve any of "the least of these" we are actually serving Christ himself. Love is the mark of true believers. But even that love comes from God:
We love because he first loved us. (1 John 4:19)

TOPICS: Compassion, consequences, faith, God's kingdom, Heaven, Hell, judgment

**MEMORY
SPARKS:**   To find yourself in this story, think of a time when . . .
1. Someone showed you a great kindness, but they can't even remember it now . . .
2. Someone thanked you for something you don't even remember doing . . .
3. You realized you'd met Jesus in disguise . . .

To help your students connect with this story, say, "Think of a time when . . ."
1. You knew someone needed your help, and you thought about helping her, but didn't . . . What happened?
2. You saw a little act of kindness go a long way . . .
3. You passed by someone in need and told yourself, *Someone else will stop to help him* . . . What happened?

HERE'S WHAT'S GOING ON:

Jesus told this story in the context of talking about the last days and his final return. He has just told three stories about being ready for his return. The parables of "The Unfaithful Servant" (Matthew 24:45-51) and "The Ten Bridesmaids" (Matthew 25:1-13) emphasize the importance of being alert and prepared. The story of "The Servants and the Bags of Gold" (Matthew 25:14-30) emphasizes the importance of being faithful in using the gifts that God has given us.

As you may recall, all of these stories were prompted by the disciples' request in Matthew 24:3: *"As Jesus was sitting on the Mount of Olives, the disciples came to him privately. 'Tell us,' they said, 'when will this happen, and what will be the sign of your coming and of the end of the age?'"*

Now, at last, Jesus closes up this storytelling session with his famous story of "The Sheep and the Goats."

HERE'S WHAT THE STORY'S ABOUT:

When Jesus returns to judge the world, he'll separate the believers from the unbelievers. Lives of compassion marked by the presence of the Holy Spirit will be evident to him, but those people without renewed minds and hearts will also be evident to him. Unbelievers will be sent away from him to eternal punishment, but the righteous will receive eternal life.

Several of Jesus' other stories are similar to this one in their description of the judgment, the separation of believers from unbelievers, and the final destination of those being judged. (See "The Seeds and the Weeds" [Matthew 13:24-30, 36-43] and "The Net" [Matthew 13:47-50].)

A couple aspects of the parable of "The Sheep and the Goats" make it unique. First, Jesus emphasized that the righteous and the unrighteous will lead different types of lives. The righteous will lead compassionate, sacrificial lives, and the unrighteous will not.

Second, believers didn't even notice their own compassion, and the unbelievers didn't notice their own lack of compassion.

> *They* [the unrighteous] *also will answer, "Lord, when did we see you hungry or thirsty or a stranger or needing clothes or sick or in prison, and did not help you?" He will reply, "I tell you the truth, whatever you did not do for one of the least of these, you did not do for me."*　　　　　　　(Matthew 25:44, 45)

The third unique aspect of this story is the mystery of compassion: when we help those in need and show our love in practical ways, we're actually offering that service not just to others, but to Jesus himself!

The point of this story is not that we get to Heaven because of the good works that we do. (We know from Ephesians 2:8, 9 that we're saved solely through God's grace, and not because of our own efforts at all—see also Romans 11:6.) Rather, the point of this story is that our lives will be changed by our faith, and that we will show compassion in practical ways. And even when we don't notice it, God does.

Caring for "the least of these" should be the blueprint for our lives.

QuickTip #42 - Help Your Stories S.O.A.R.!
To help your stories reach the hearts and minds of young children, fill your stories with **S**ounds (music, rhymes, chants, singing, sound effects), **O**bjects (props, toys, felt-board figures, crafts), **A**ctions (gestures, finger plays, creative dramatics), and **R**epetition (refrains, responses, cyclical stories).

If you do, your stories will SOAR!

TELLING THIS STORY TO STUDENTS AGES 3-7

The Ugly Little *Sheep*ling?!

For this lesson, you may wish to begin by telling the children a version of the Hans Christian Andersen story, "The Ugly Duckling." In his **fable**, a swan grows up with some ducks. He feels rejected and sad because he thinks he's the ugliest and clumsiest of all. But all the while, he's really growing into a beautiful swan! In the end, his true identity is revealed, and he goes to live with the beautiful creatures whom he has always admired.

In the same way, in the end we'll all be revealed for who we truly are. God knows who the sheep and the goats are. He sees into our hearts. And in the final scene of the story of the earth, God will bring all who trust in him home to live happily ever after.

Then briefly retell Jesus' story in your own words. Here is a sample of what you might say:

> **Kids, long ago, Jesus told a story about when he's going to come back. When he does, he'll be surrounded by angels! And he'll separate the Christians from all those who don't believe in him.**
>
> **He'll come as a king on a great throne.**
>
> **Then, Jesus will tell all the Christians that they can come to Heaven. (Now, Jesus called the Christians sheep because he's like a shepherd who watches over us.)**
>
> **He'll tell them, "Come be with me! For you fed me and helped me and visited me in the hospital or in jail, and you were kind to me and took care of me!"**
>
> **But they'll say, "When did we do all that for you?"**
>
> **And Jesus will say, "When you did it for others, you did it for me."**
>
> **Jesus called the unbelievers goats because they don't listen to him. He won't bring them to be with him in Heaven. He'll tell them, "You didn't feed me when I was hungry, or help me when I was hurt, or take care of me at all!"**
>
> **And they'll say, "When did we fail to do that for you?"**
>
> **Jesus will answer, "When you failed to love others, you failed to love me."**
>
> **Then he'll bring all the Christians home to a new life in Heaven that never ends.**

After telling your story, review the story with the following **story dramatization**. The underlined words are cues to have your students perform the indicated action.

OK, kids, let's pretend that we're the different people and objects from this story . . . First, let's pretend that we're <u>angels</u>, flying around the throne of God! Show me your mighty angel wings! Good job . . . Now, Jesus is the King of kings! He rules everything! Let's all pretend that we're <u>kings</u> or <u>queens</u>. Find a throne and sit down and put on your crown . . .

Now, let's pretend that we're the Christians, the <u>sheep</u>! Everybody become a sheep . . . Good! . . . Now, let's change into those naughty <u>goats</u>! Show me some naughty, mean goat faces . . .

Wow! Good! Then the king talked about being <u>hungry</u> . . . show me what you look like when you're hungry . . . or <u>thirsty</u> . . . or <u>sick</u> . . . or in <u>jail</u> . . . would you be scared in jail? . . . What if you didn't have a home? Would you be happy or sad if you were homeless? . . . What about if you <u>didn't have any clothes!</u> Ah!

Now, <u>share some food</u> . . . and <u>cans of soda</u> . . . and <u>clothes</u> . . . <u>Give someone a hug!</u>

Good! Then Jesus invited all the Christians to be with him forever in Heaven. And they were <u>happy</u>! But he had to send all the unbelievers away, and they were <u>sad</u> . . .

I'd rather be <u>happy</u>, wouldn't you?

Let's all remember that if we love Jesus, we need to show it by loving and being kind to other people! The end!

To close up your lesson, sing a few verses from the following **song**. Make up your own fun actions to the song, and remember that each time through, you repeat all the previous refrains and gestures!

He'll Be Landin' on a Mountain When He Comes
(sing to the tune of "She'll Be Comin' Round the Mountain")

He'll be <u>landin' on a mountain</u> when he comes . . .
(Jump up and down and say, "Oof! Oof!")
He'll be <u>landin' on a mountain</u> when he comes . . .
(Say, "Oof! Oof!")
He'll be <u>landin' on a mountain</u>,
He'll be <u>landin' on a mountain</u>,
He'll be <u>landin' on a mountain</u> when he comes . . .
(Say, "Oof! Oof!")

He'll be <u>ridin' on a big throne</u> when he comes . . .
(Wave your arm and say [like a cowboy], "Yee-haw!")

And we'll <u>all bow down to meet him</u> when he comes . . .
(Bow down low and say, "Hi, there!")

And he'll <u>separate the people</u> when he comes . . .
(Gesture with your hands and say, "Sort, sort!")

And we'll <u>all be shocked to see him</u> when he comes . . .
(Look surprised and say, "Whoa, dude!")

And the <u>goats will all be sent away for good</u> . . .
(Wave good-bye and say, "Bye, goats!")

And the <u>sheep will join the party</u> when he comes . . .
(Cheer and say, "Hooray!")

	Creative Connection Section	
Field Trip Ideas	Go to a park where homeless people live, or get cardboard boxes and sit in them as you tell the story. Have the students try to imagine living in a box!	
Mood and Atmosphere	This story is full of surprises. There's also joy for the sheep and despair for the goats.	
Sensory Connections	Sight and Touch	In this story, Jesus emphasizes how important it is for believers to meet physical needs. Explore food, drink, clothing, bandages and other items that relate to the needy people Jesus listed. If you use props, pull them out of a first aid kit!
	Hearing	The camp song, "I Just Wanna Be a Sheep" would be a fun song to use for this lesson, especially with the younger children.
	Taste	Make little sheep and goats out of marshmallows and straight pretzels. Put eyes on them with a little frosting and small pieces of candy. Put little horns on the goats. When you're done with the story, eat the goats!
	Smell	As you tell this story, sort your laundry and show where the clean clothes (sheep) go, and where the dirty clothes (goats) go. Some peoples' choices and lives are dirty and stinky; others have been washed clean by Christ!
Costume Ideas	You could dress up like a sheep by wearing a wool sweater to tell this story! You could also dress up like a homeless person or a prisoner and share a monologue!	

W.E.G.I. (Weird & Extremely Goofy Ideas)

In the parallel parable of "The Net" (Matthew 13:47-50), Jesus talked about throwing away the bad fish. Bring a rotten fish and talk about how much lives without compassion stink to God!

TELLING THIS STORY TO STUDENTS AGES 8-12

One memorable way to retell this story is to have someone read the story right out of the Bible while you have actors simply lounging around eating munchies and drinking soda while watching TV until, at the end, they finally fall asleep.

The contrast between the sacrificial compassion talked about in the story and the typical laziness and self-indulgence of modern life will be very powerful.[1]

Here's an animated **progressive** way to retell this story for your preteens.

Rockin' to the Sheep Beat
(a progressive rhythmic version of "The Sheep and the Goats")

Notes for the storytellers: You'll need 6 performers for this story. Before beginning, call them up and let them practice their parts. Consider writing the words on note cards so they can rehearse them easier.

Practice by yourself to make sure you're comfortable hearing the rhythms and weaving the refrains into a round. Explain that everyone will stop doing their part whenever you raise both hands. Then, tell the story and add the groups one at a time, as directed below (you will be the NARRATOR).

NARRATOR: **Jesus said that at the end of time, when he returns, he'll separate all the people—the unbelievers on his left, and the believers on his right.**

PERSON #1: *(animated, with gestures and rhythm)* **"You go here and you go there and do not try to switch! . . . You go here and you go there and do not try to switch! . . ."**

NARRATOR: **He'll invite the believers to come home with him to Heaven! And he'll say, "When I was hungry and thirsty, you took good care of me!"**

PERSON #2: *(smiling, rubbing your tummy, with rhythm)* **"Mac and cheese, mac and cheese, tastin' really good, mmm! . . . Mac and cheese, mac and cheese, tastin' really good, mmm! . . ."** *(repeat until NARRATOR stops you)*

(PERSON #1 joins in after PERSON #2 has said her part twice. Repeat until NARRATOR stops you.)

NARRATOR: **And when I was sick or in the hospital or in jail, you came and visited me!**

PERSON #3: *(smiling, with rhythm)* **"Look! I brought you flowers just to brighten up your room! . . . Look! I brought you flowers just to brighten up your room! . . ."** *(repeat until Narrator stops you)*

(PERSON #2 joins in after PERSON #3 has said her part twice. Then PERSON #1 joins . . . Repeat until NARRATOR stops you.)

NARRATOR: **And when I was naked, you gave me clothes!**

PERSON #4: *(cover yourself as if you have no clothes on, with rhythm)* **"Ah! . . . Don't look! . . . Just get a towel quick! . . . Ah! . . . Don't look! . . . Just get a towel quick! . . ."** *(repeat until NARRATOR stops you)*

(previous PERSONS join in as before . . . repeat until NARRATOR stops you)

NARRATOR: **But they won't understand! They'll say, "When did we treat you so kindly?" And he'll say . . .**

[1] This idea is based on the drama sketch "The Sheep, the Goats, and Larry" found in my book *Worship Sketches 2 Perform* (Meriwether Publishing, 2001). This script appears on pages 214–216.

PERSON #5: *(rapping, with rhythm)* **"Whenever you were kind to others, you were kind to me! . . . Whenever you were kind to others, you were kind to me! . . ."**
(repeat until NARRATOR stops you)

(previous PERSONS join in as before . . . repeat until NARRATOR stops you)

NARRATOR: **And then he'll turn to the unbelievers and tell them, "Get away from me! For when I was in need, you didn't help me at all." So then, he'll tell the unbelievers to go away to be with the devil and his demons, but he'll invite the believers to come home with him to Heaven!**

PERSON #6: *(singing enthusiastically, with rhythm)* **"Ha-a-llelujah! We're finally home! . . . Ha-a-llelujah! We're finally home! . . ."** *(repeat until NARRATOR stops you)*

(previous PERSONS join as before . . . repeat until NARRATOR stops you)

NARRATOR: **The end!**

After telling this story, use **Scripture snapshots** to review the different scenes from the story. Assign the scenes listed below to groups of 3-5 students. Don't let the other groups know what each assignment is! Keep it a secret!

Then have the students guess which scenes the other groups are portraying.
1. The arrival of the king. (Matthew 25:31, 32)
2. The king separating the goats from the sheep. (Matthew 25:32, 33)
3. The naked king getting some clothes. (Matthew 25:36)
4. The hungry king not getting any food. (Matthew 25:42)
5. The surprised unbelievers when they realized they hadn't shown compassion. (Matthew 25:44-46)

Preteen girls are often getting interested in cheerleading, chants, and cheers. Have them create their own cheer (words and actions) based on this story. Or, use the suggested **rhyme** below and have them develop a cheer that they can perform for one of the younger classes!

Get down! Get with it!
Get Jesus in your life!
He lived and died and rose
So you can live and die and rise!

Get down! Get with it!
He paid, he paid the price.
He gave his life upon the cross
As a sacrifice.

Get down! Get with it!
Get rid of all that pride.
There's nothing you can do without him,
Even if you try.

Get down! Get with it!
And stare into the Light!
He brought you back, so back him up,
And live your life for Christ!

Counting Sheep
(a fill-in version of "The Sheep and the Goats")

Notes for the storyteller: REMEMBER NOT TO REVEAL WHICH STORY YOU'RE STUDYING! Just gather suggestions from the audience and write the words on the blanks within the story. Then read and enjoy!

When you're done, review the Bible story to see how close to (or far away from) your version it was!
This is the story of "The Sheep and the Goats."
Jesus told this story long ago . . .

At the end of time when the chief _____ arrives, sitting on his great
(a very important job)

heavenly _____, he'll separate all the believers on his right and all the
(a type of furniture)

unbelievers on his left. Just like separating _____ from the
(a type of unusual animal)

_____.
(another type of unusual animal)

Then he will turn to those on his right, to the believers, and say, "_____!
(a popular saying)

Come and _____ with me! Here is your inheritance, just like I promised. Here's
(something to do that's fun)

your reward: a _____ and _____!
(something cool you might buy at the mall)   *(something very, very expensive)*

"For when I was hungry, you gave me _____ and _____. When I
(a type of food)   *(another type of food)*

was thirsty you gave me something to drink! When I was a stranger you

_____! When I was sick and in prison, you _____!"
(a kind thing to do)   *(something your parents are always asking you to do)*

But they'll say, "But when?! When did we do all those kind things to you?"

And he'll say, "I tell you, whatever you have done for _____ you have
(the name of a group of people)

done for me!"

Then he will turn to the unbelievers and say, "Get away from me! I'm sending you down
into the fiery pits of _____!
(a place you wouldn't want to visit)

"For when I was hungry, you gave me nothin'! Not even _____. When I was
(a gross type of food)

thirsty or sick or in prison, you didn't help. When I had no home or no clothes, you didn't

help. Instead you _____!"
(something mean to do to someone)

But they'll say, "_____! When?! When did we fail to do all those
(a saying from California)

kind things to you?"

"I tell you, whatever you have failed to do for the least of these brothers and sisters of
mine, you have failed to do for me."

Then he'll send them away to spend forever with demons, but he'll invite all of the
believers to come home with him to _____.
(a cool place you've always wanted to go)

The end.

PRAYER CONNECTION:

1. Pray for those who are poor, alone, hurting, or helpless.
2. Pray for the eyes to see people's needs and the courage to help others selflessly.
3. Pray for forgiveness for failing to show the compassion that God has called us each to have.

INTERACTIVE PRAYER IDEA:

Lead a responsive prayer. After you read each line, the students respond by saying together,
"Help me live a life of love."

Show me the way, Lord. Show me the way. *"Help me live a life of love."*
Teach me to follow. Teach me how to obey. *"Help me live a life of love."*
As I learn to walk by faith, as I walk with you today; *"Help me live a life of love."*
Show me the way. Show me the way. Show me the way, I pray. *"Help me live a life of love."*
Amen.

APPENDIX A - SCRIPTURE VERSE INDEX

Appendix B - Topical Index

Boldness
The Friend in the Night

Compassion
The Good Samaritan
The Sheep and the Goats

Complaining
The Workers in the Field

Confession
The Two Men Who Prayed

Consequences
The Unmerciful Servant
The Foolish Rich Man
The Ten Bridesmaids
The Servants and the Bags of Gold
The Sheep and the Goats

Distractions
The Sower and the Four Soils
The Foolish Rich Man
The Great Banquet
The Ten Bridesmaids

Envy
The Workers in the Field

Evangelism
(see Witnessing)

Excuses
The Great Banquet

Faith
The Sower and the Four Soils
The Friend in the Night
Lost and Found (Three Stories in One!)
Lazarus and the Rich Man
The Vineyard and the Farmers
The Ten Bridesmaids
The Sheep and the Goats

Faithfulness
The Servants and the Bags of Gold

Fear
The Servants and the Bags of Gold

Following God
The Wise and Foolish Builders

Forgiveness
The Unmerciful Servant
Lost and Found (Three Stories in One!)
The Two Men Who Prayed

Giftedness
The Servants and the Bags of Gold

God's Character
The Friend in the Night
The Great Banquet
Lost and Found (Three Stories in One!)

God's Kingdom
The Sower and the Four Soils
The Unmerciful Servant
The Great Banquet
Lost and Found (Three Stories in One!)
The Workers in the Field
The Vineyard and the Farmers
The Ten Bridesmaids
The Servants and the Bags of Gold
The Sheep and the Goats

God's Word
The Wise and Foolish Builders
Lazarus and the Rich Man

Grace
The Unmerciful Servant
Lost and Found (Three Stories in One!)
The Workers in the Field

Greed
The Foolish Rich Man

Grudges
The Unmerciful Servant

Heaven
The Good Samaritan
Lazarus and the Rich Man
The Workers in the Field
The Sheep and the Goats

Hell
Lazarus and the Rich Man
The Sheep and the Goats

Holy Spirit
The Friend in the Night

Humility
The Two Men Who Prayed

Hypocrisy
The Wise and Foolish Builders
The Two Men Who Prayed

Israel
The Vineyard and the Farmers

Judgment
The Unmerciful Servant
The Foolish Rich Man
Lazarus and the Rich Man
The Ten Bridesmaids
The Sheep and the Goats

Justice
Lazarus and the Rich Man

Love
The Good Samaritan

Materialism
The Sower and the Four Soils
The Foolish Rich Man
Lazarus and the Rich Man
The Vineyard and the Farmers

Mercy
The Unmerciful Servant
The Good Samaritan

Obedience
The Wise and Foolish Builders

Patience
The Ten Bridesmaids

Persecution
The Wise and Foolish Builders
The Sower and the Four Soils
The Vineyard and the Farmers

Perseverance
The Wise and Foolish Builders
The Sower and the Four Soils
The Ten Bridesmaids

Persistence
The Friend in the Night

Pharisees
The Foolish Rich Man
The Great Banquet
Lost and Found (Three Stories in One!)
The Two Men Who Prayed
The Vineyard and the Farmers

Prayer
The Friend in the Night
The Two Men Who Prayed

Prejudice
The Good Samaritan

Preparedness
The Ten Bridesmaids

Pride
The Two Men Who Prayed

Priorities
The Good Samaritan
The Foolish Rich Man
The Great Banquet
Lazarus and the Rich Man
The Ten Bridesmaids
The Servants and the Bags of Gold

Repentance
Lost and Found (Three Stories in One!)

Resentment
The Workers in the Field

Responsibilities
The Servants and the Bags of Gold

Rewards
The Workers in the Field
The Servants and the Bags of Gold

Righteousness
Lazarus and the Rich Man

Risk-Taking
The Servants and the Bags of Gold

Showing Off
The Two Men Who Prayed

Sin
Lost and Found (Three Stories in One!)
The Two Men Who Prayed

Stubbornness
The Two Men Who Prayed

Unforgiveness
The Unmerciful Servant

Wealth
The Foolish Rich Man
Lazarus and the Rich Man

Wisdom
The Wise and Foolish Builders

Witnessing
The Sower and the Four Soils
The Great Banquet
Lazarus and the Rich Man

APPENDIX C - STORYTELLING TECHNIQUE INDEX

Add-on Storytelling
Lost and Found (Three Stories in One!)
The Servants and the Bags of Gold

Call and Response Storytelling
The Wise and Foolish Builders .
The Good Samaritan
The Workers in the Field

Contemporary Retelling
The Sower and the Four Soils
The Friend in the Night
The Great Banquet
Lost and Found (Three Stories in One!)
The Two Men Who Prayed
The Workers in the Field
The Vineyard and the Farmers

Fill-In Storytelling
Lost and Found (Three Stories in One!)
The Two Men Who Prayed
The Sheep and the Goats

Finger Plays & Gestures
The Good Samaritan

Folktales & Fables
The Good Samaritan
The Friend in the Night
The Foolish Rich Man
The Great Banquet
Lazarus and the Rich Man
The Two Men Who Prayed
The Workers in the Field
The Servants and the Bags of Gold
The Sheep and the Goats

Games
The Sower and the Four Souls
Lost and Found (Three Stories in One!)
The Workers in the Field

Group Refrain Story
The Wise and Foolish Builders
The Unmerciful Servant
Lazarus and the Rich Man
The Vineyard and the Farmers

Human Clay
The Ten Bridesmaids

Imaginary Journey
The Wise and Foolish Builders
The Friend in the Night

Improvisational Role-Playing
The Wise and Foolish Builders
The Good Samaritan

Masks
The Unmerciful Servant
Lazarus and the Rich Man

Monologues
The Good Samaritan
The Friend in the Night
Lost and Found (Three Stories in One!)
The Servants and the Bags of Gold

Narrative Pantomime
The Wise and Foolish Builders
The Sower and the Four Soils
The Vineyard and the Farmers
The Ten Bridesmaids

Organic Storytelling
The Great Banquet
Lost and Found (Three Stories in One!)

Progressive Storytelling
The Sheep and the Goats

Props
The Unmerciful Servant
The Foolish Rich Man
Lost and Found (Three Stories in One!)
The Ten Bridesmaids

Puppet Scripts
(see Reader's Theatre Scripts and Tandem Storytelling)

Rap/Rhyming Storytelling
The Ten Bridesmaids
The Sheep and the Goats

Reader's Theatre Scripts
The Wise and Foolish Builders
The Unmerciful Servant
The Workers in the Field
The Vineyard and the Farmers
The Servants and the Bags of Gold

Rebus
The Foolish Rich Man

Scripture Snapshots
Lost and Found (Three Stories in One!)
The Sheep and the Goats

Signal Card Storytelling
The Great Banquet

Skits
(see also Reader's Theatre Scripts)
The Good Samaritan
The Friend in the Night

Songs
The Wise and Foolish Builders
The Sower and the Four Soils
The Workers in the Field
The Sheep and the Goats

Sound Effects
The Wise and Foolish Builders
Lost and Found (Three Stories in One!)

Story Bag
(see also Props)
The Sower and the Four Soils

Story Dramatization
The Sower and the Four Soils
The Foolish Rich Man
Lazarus and the Rich Man
The Two Men Who Prayed
The Servants and the Bags of Gold
The Sheep and the Goats

Storymime
The Wise and Foolish Builders
Lost and Found (Three Stories in One!)
The Two Men Who Prayed

Tandem Monologues
The Wise and Foolish Builders
Lazarus and the Rich Man

Tandem Storytelling
The Great Banquet

"What If?" Storytelling
The Good Samaritan